From Selma to Salvation

Junnus Clay, Jr

"My Spiritual Journey from Activism to Evangelism"

with Lessons Learned

RDS Publications
Marietta, Georgia

From Selma to Salvation

Testimonials

"From Selma to Salvation – provides a heartfelt, poignant and powerful perspective. One feels the pain and power through one man's story of a special time and place in our nation's history. It's about everyday heroes among us. Read it. Learn it. Live it. Be awed and be inspired. Then start walking...and bring someone with you." – *Tom Stokes, Commercial Real Estate Broker, Atlanta, GA*

"FROM SELMA TO SALVATION – is not a stale. stagnant presentation. Rather it is an action-packed cataloging of a movement... an eyewitness account...The author moves from bitterness to betterment. Bitterness towards the white instigators of Bloody Sunday is irradicated as the grace of God leads him to salvation through the preaching of a white clergyman. It's hard not to read the book through in one sitting." – *Dr. W. Charles Lewis, Pastor, Dothan, AL*

"*From Selma to Salvation* – is a fact-filled slice of Americana, an eyewitness account that epitomizes the impact of racism at ground zero. This is a must read, it lays bare one of the tenets of Critical Race Theory, how racism affects outcomes. – *Elington Bates, Minister, Roswell, GA*

From Selma to Salvation

From Selma to Salvation

© 2015
by
Junnus Clay, Jr

Scripture taken from the HOLY BIBLE INTERNATIONAL VERSION, copyright
© 1973, 1978, 1984 by International Bible Society. Used by permission of
Zondervan Publishing House. All rights reserved.

Printed in the United States of America

First Printing 2015, Second Printing 2017, Third Printing 2018,
Fourth Printing 2021

ISBN 978-0-692-38818-1

Library of Congress Control Number: 2015933842

RDS Publications
2615 George Busbee Parkway, Suite 11-343
Kennesaw, GA 30144
email: jclay128@gmail.com / phone: (678) 386-8648

To purchase additional copies of the book: call or email us, or go
to www.amazon.com

Dedications

This is a small book, but it covers a life journey of 50 years. During this time many good people crossed my path, and touched my life. I thank God for each of them. This book is dedicated to them. Some of their names are mentioned in the book, so I will not repeat them here.

To those special people who have loved and supported me unconditionally for a lifetime:

In Loving Memory of:
Leola Clay
Betty Faye Whitlow-Clay
Bonnie Jean Anderson-Clay
Pastor Lecester Strong

My Three Children:
Davida, Claressa and Simeon

My Four Siblings:
Vivian, Joe, Diane, and Benita

To three special people who have brought new joy into my life and family:

Phyllis Scott Clay
Nicholas Andrew Clay (grandson #1)
Dylan Jackson (grandson # 2)

From Selma to Salvation

To Pastor Jerald Stallworth and the members of Selma
Community Bible Church

*for being faithful in proclaiming the Word of God, and
continuing to serve the Lord in spite of unusual hardships,
suffering and loss.*

To the Unsung Heroes of the Selma Civil Rights Movement:

*Ellis Charles Quarles (Pee Wee) - my cousin - a Foot Soldier of
Bloody Sunday - (deceased 2007)*

*All of the people who participated in the 1965 Selma Movement,
made sacrifices, have never been recognized by name, and have
never received any rewards or accolades.*

*My classmates, the students of R. B. Hudson High School, who
stayed out of school, participated in the marches, and went to
jail.*

Content

Preface

It has been over 47 years since I left Selma, Alabama at the age of 17. However, since leaving I have returned home many times, and for many events. Most of them were pleasant visits.

As I started to write this life journey, I made several discoveries:

- *Three recent events prompted me to write about my Selma journey now: (1) last year (2013), I was moved to find and express gratitude to Pastor Roy Edgemon who led me to Christ in 1973, (2) to leave a legacy for my children and grandchildren, (3) the new "Selma" movie, it was a great production; it helped to re-instill some pride within myself for a hometown that I was ashamed of during my younger years.*

- *All of the events, I cite and refer to in this book are true. They actually happened and I was actually there. However, since I was so young, 14 years old, and the Selma events occurred over 50 years ago, I used several Civil Rights authors' books for reference. I acknowledge these authors in the reference section of this book.*

- *Recalling and writing about these experiences caused unexpected "emotions and weeping" at times. It appears that for emotional protection, I had locked out of my mind the memories of the most traumatic events.*

- My purpose and goals for this book are:

    (1) to inspire faith in God, and celebrate the history of

my people and our common struggle for justice and equality in America.

(2) to celebrate the unsung heroes (the students and residents of Selma who participated in the marches) of the Selma Movement most of whose names and pictures have never appeared in a book, newspaper or magazine. These unsung heroes never sought praise or recognition for their service and sacrifices. They were just humble people who answered the call of history to risk their lives and livelihood to "stand up for a cause greater than themselves."

(3) to express thanks, appreciation and gratitude to the many people who God allowed to touch my life "for good" along the 50-year journey covered in this book.

(4) to hopefully inspire a new generation of young people (especially African-Americans): (a) to discover and commit their lives to "a cause greater than themselves." (b) to study and learn the history of our people. (c) to appreciate and show gratitude for those who "suffered and died" to insure that each new generation of Americans (of all ethnicities) have the opportunity to live "the Dream" that Dr. King spoke about and died for.

February 10, 2015
Marietta, Georgia

Introduction

In March 1973, I found myself, a young 23 year old black man from Selma, Alabama, who had marched in the Civil Rights Movement with Dr. Martin L. King in 1965, who had been beaten and tear gassed by Alabama state troopers on Bloody Sunday, sitting in a revival meeting listening to a white southern Baptist preacher in a church in Yokohama, Japan. Does this story sound too good to be true? Hold on! It gets better! At the end of the revival meeting that night in 1973, following the white preacher's instruction, I went home, got on my knees, prayed the sinner's prayer, "asked the Lord Jesus Christ to forgive my sins, to save me, and give me eternal life."

For 42 years since that night, I have been studying, teaching, and preaching the Gospel of Jesus Christ, and leading other people to Christ just like that white southern Baptist preacher did for me, and starting new churches across America.

I finally met that preacher, Rev. Roy Edgemon, 41 years later (2014), in Atlanta, Georgia. I told him about how God used his sermon that night to lead me to salvation, that I had been a minister for 37 years, and later I started a new Bible teaching church, Selma Community Bible Church, back in my hometown of Selma, Alabama. For 41 years Pastor Roy never knew the impact of the sermon he preached that night. I thanked him for being faithful to his calling and I treated him to lunch. We spent several hours talking, reminiscing and thanking God for His goodness and favor in both our lives and ministries.

The point of this story and the purpose of this book are to take you, the reader, on an exciting journey and tell you the marvelous story of how the power of the Gospel and the love of

From Selma to Salvation

Jesus Christ enabled me to overcome racial, class, and social barriers. In spite of the racial hatred I experienced at the hand of white segregationists growing up in Selma, and regardless of the anger I personally carried as a result of experiencing degrading treatment during the Civil Rights Movement. After accepting Christ's love and forgiveness for my sins, I was able to forgive the white racists of Selma for the sinful acts of violence, segregation and discrimination that they perpetuated against me, and other African-Americans. This deliverance does not make me special or favored, many others have found the same type of spiritual freedom after receiving Jesus Christ as their Savior.

"So in Christ you are all children of God...There is neither Jew nor Gentile, neither slave nor free, nor is there male or female, for you all are one in Christ Jesus. If you belong to Christ, then you are all heirs according to the promise." (Galatians 3:26-29)

My Invitation to You:

If you have never accepted Christ as your Lord and Savior for the forgiveness of your sins, and do not have the assurance of eternal life in heaven when you die, I invite to you do so now. Pray and ask Jesus Christ, by faith to save you, then find a good church to attend (Ephesians 2:8, 9; Romans 10: 9, 10).

Lessons Learned

Always be open to hear from God; never limit or restrict Him in your life. Holding on to prejudices can hinder God's blessings in your life. Remember, he can use anyone, at any time, in any place to bless you.

From Selma to Salvation

Chapter One

Growing Up in Selma

Prior to 1965 Selma, Alabama was a quiet, small, segregated town in central Alabama with a population of about 20,000 people. Being the largest city, and the county seat of Dallas County many people from the surrounding rural towns and counties came to Selma on a weekly basis to shop, socialize and conduct business. The city and county populations have always been majority black. Within the city limits there were two high schools, one black (R.B. Hudson), and one white (Parrish High). Segregation was the normal way of life prior to the 1960s. African-Americans accepted it, and whites comfortably enjoyed it. I would only later learn how vested the white establishment was in enforcing and maintaining segregation as the "law of the land."

In spite of growing up in segregated schools, I did not feel deprived educationally, because my teachers were all college trained, and they took a personal interest in my life and learning. I was a good student, but I do remember getting "hand paddled" once by my teacher, Ms. Bradford, for missing a homework assignment in history class; Chief Williams drove me home once to talk with my Mom about joining the band; and when I would spend my bus money on snacks, Ms. Jones, my home room teacher gave me 25 cents for bus fare on more than one occasion. Our teachers cared about us as people. l would not have had that kind of support in an integrated school setting in Alabama during the 1960s. Nevertheless, forced segregation was a violation of our Civil Rights, and it was wrong.

I vividly remember the separate black and white water fountains in the S.S. Kress department store, and sitting in the all black balcony section of both the Walton and Wilby movie theaters. As a teenager, I did not ride the city bus, I owned a

14

bike, but I remember seeing black adults getting on the bus at the back door and sitting in the back. I was too young to understand the politics and the disadvantages of blacks not being able to vote. But to me, the most obvious signs of segregation and discrimination against blacks in Selma was "poverty." Black housing and black neighborhoods in Selma were for many people, inadequate and sub-standard. Unpaved streets and shotgun houses without indoor plumbing or running water was the norm for many black homes. Especially in east Selma, where I lived and grew up. As I grew older, I spent more time away from home staying with my Aunt Etta in west Selma because she lived in a better neighborhood than we did, even though her family had less income.

I was more disgusted by the poverty conditions of living in Selma than the institutional racism. Though I would later understand that the two were linked together. My father (Junnus Clay, Sr.) died in 1953 at age 30 of injuries he sustained as a soldier in the U.S. Army. I was only two years old at the time. From that point, my Mom (Leola Clay) and all four (4) children received Veteran Administration (VA) benefits. As a family, we literally had more financial stability than many other black families in Selma, but our living conditions did not reflect this fact. We actually could have afforded to live in a better house and a better community than east Selma. But two factors hindered us: 1) my mom had a large extended family that she loved, and she was very generous in helping them in times of need. 2) She was not knowledgeable about all the VA benefits that were available to us as a family. My family did not move out of east Selma into adequate housing until 1973, by this time I had already left home, graduated from college, and obtained a professional job. In fact I sent Mom the down payment on the new HUD house.

From Selma to Salvation

My maternal family migrated into Selma from Tyler, which is 12 miles east of Selma on Highway 80. Both my parents were descendants from farmers and worked domestic, labor, or farm related jobs. Nevertheless, my mother was determined about her children getting an education. This was the one VA benefit that she understood very well. And like many other black parents, she firmly believed that education was our one way ticket out of poverty and the injustice of racial discrimination.

The one phrase she often repeated from my elementary years in school was: *"your daddy left some money up there for y'all; y'all better go up there and get it!"* It wasn't until I took a VA college enrollment test as a high school senior that I finally understood what she meant by "the money daddy had left for us" was a tuition free college education, plus a monthly room and board allowance. In this respect, I was very fortunate compared to many other black youth growing up in Selma. This reality hit home one semester when I sadly witnessed one of my Selma classmates withdrawing from college to go home because he had no money. I lost my dad, but I had access to a free college education. I never had an opportunity to know my dad, but according to my mother, and his family members he was a good man. She always spoke endearingly about him, and referred to him by the nick name "Bae." He was the oldest son of six siblings in the Smith and Ruby Clay clan. In his absence, my paternal family members were very kind to us. I enjoyed going to Tyler to visit them during the summers as a child.

On the education point my mother was right. Education was instrumental in helping to lift me and my family out of poverty, even though the equal rights legislations were slow to be enacted. I and five of my high school classmates enrolled in Alabama A&M College in 1968 after graduating from high school.

From Selma to Salvation

Church Life

During my years growing up in Selma, my family held membership at Mt. Ararat Baptist Church in east Selma. The church was on Division Street, the same street where I lived, about 10 blocks away. I was a regular attender at both Sunday School and church services. I descended from a family with a long-standing church heritage. My maternal grandfather, Alexander Calhoun, was a life-long deacon at the rural, New Liberty Baptist church in Tyler, where both my dad and mom families originated. Therefore, church attendance was mandatory. Again, I was blessed in this respect, because the foundation of church life and respect for God was laid early in my life.

At about the age of 12, I was baptized and became an official member of the church. Pastor Harrison, Sister Annie Ruth Huckabee and the adult members of our church were very affirming and supportive of us as youth in the church. Several of my high school classmates attended the same church: Ronald Hatcher, Cora Thomas, Roy Johnson, Patricia Mack and Rio Brooks. But beyond doing the socially acceptable thing of getting baptized and becoming a member, I do not recall having a spiritual experience of any kind, or receiving any instructions about salvation, baptism, or accepting Jesus Christ as one's Savior. It appeared that baptismal regeneration was a standard practice in black churches at that time. The Sunday sermons were loud, long, dramatized speeches that contained many positive statements about the goodness, power and attributes of God but the hooping, hollering, sweating, and shouting made it all unintelligible to me as young person. By the time I entered high school my interest in attending church was waning. After I left home in the fall of 1968 heading to college, my church attendance literally stopped.

Lessons Learned

1. *Growing up with faith in God, good morals and strong family values are more important than growing up with financial wealth. Money can be earned during one's lifetime, but if a person grows up without a foundation of spiritual and moral values, successful living can be difficult.*

2. *"Train up a child in the way that he should go; even when he is old he will not depart from it." (Proverbs 22:6)*

3. *I am convinced that many of the social problems we experience in American society today are rooted in the fact that God and church attendance are either absent or optional in many families.*

Chapter Two

The Civil Rights Movement Comes to Selma

Sometime in 1964, mass meetings began in Selma. By 1965 when I started attending, the meetings were held at two churches: Brown Chapel AME and First Baptist, both located on Sylvan Street, just two blocks apart. As the crowds attending the meeting grew larger, on some occasions two separate meetings were held on the same night. The adults met at Brown Chapel and the youth met at First Baptist. The keynote speakers usually came and spoke to both groups. The speakers ranged from local pastors, SCLC/SNCC organizers and leaders to black activists who were gaining national notoriety in the movement. They included: John Lewis, James Bevel, C.T. Vivian, Fred Shuttlesworth, Rev. F. D. Reese, Malcom X, Hosea Williams, Andrew Young. Dr. Martin L. King Jr. was the most coveted speaker. When he was in town, there was standing room only at both meetings. The news media usually followed Dr. King, and also occupied space in the meetings.

Usually adults filled both churches, and youth were directed to the balconies. However, as teens we didn't always enjoy the long meetings. So having no seats was at times a relief, and in between speakers we would hang around outside the church talking with friends. But, as long as seats were available, the organizers insisted that we stay inside the church during mass meetings for our own safety. The night riding KKK was not beyond doing drive by shootings or throwing gas bombs from their cars.

A group of teens (the regulars were: myself, my brother Joe, Jessie Manuel, Lee Underwood, Bobby & Arnold Thomas) from my neighborhood in east Selma usually made the 20 minute walk together to the mass meetings. We were cautioned by leaders and parents not to walk along, because white racists and KKK members, some of whom were uniformed law enforcement officers during the day, would ride the streets at night harassing blacks walking to meetings. In spite of the apparent danger, our parents still encouraged and permitted us to go.

On nights when there were no mass meetings, we would stop by the "freedom house." In east Selma, the freedom house was located in a rented house next door to Mt. Ararat Baptist Church, on Division Street. The purpose of the freedom house was to give the movement a visible presence in the community when no meetings or marches were taking place. Usually one or two community organizers were at the house for several hours, two or three nights each week. We would get updates on planned activities, and tactical training on how to fall and protect ourselves if attacked by law enforcement officers with cattle prods or billy clubs during street marches.

At other times, the freedom house became a community gathering place, primarily for youth who were involved in the movement. This gathering place was essential because during the height of the movement many students, myself included, stayed out of school for weeks at a time. At times, different students were in jail, and the freedom house became a communication center to provide information to parents about where their children were. East Selma was one of the few communities to have a freedom house because we were located a substantial distance from the headquarter churches on Sylvan Street.

From Selma to Salvation

Marching and Going to Jail

The strategy of the Selma movement leaders was to non-violently defeat the Dallas County system of government that prevented blacks from voting. By constantly demonstrating and repeatedly marching through the streets to the courthouse and attempting to register to vote; knowing that we would be denied. The objective was to exhaust the law enforcement officers and fill-up the jail space. To this end, sometimes, several marches per day would be launched from Brown Chapel Church.

I participated in multiple marches, and went to jail several times; I was arrested at least once each week during the two month period before March 1965. The typical arrest pattern was the county sheriff deputies would declare the march illegal and unauthorized without a permit. They would take away our signs, and put us on county buses, drive us to the National Guard armory, place us in a large empty room, and hold us for several hours. They would also harass and threaten us "not to march again!" We were called "niggers" so often that we became numb to the word.

This was an often repeated intimidation tactic used by the white officers, but it was not effective. We would usually be released from jail by night fall. However, some student marchers were detained for several days. Adults with cars made circuit rides by all of the local jails, so it would not be long after being released before we got picked-up outside the jail, and given a ride back to the church. We were well coached by our SNCC leaders and knew what to expect each time we went to jail. After being released, we always marched again the next day, or on the next march. Because so many of the marchers were under age kids (between the ages of 13 and 15), the authorities' options were limited by law, and there was no risk of retaliatory job loss.

Both my brother Joe and my sister Vivian also marched regularly, and they spent several days in jail at Camp Selma and Camp Camden. On one occasion, Vivian was jailed for 8 days.

Two of my high school classmates, Joe Smitherman and Lynda Blackman Lowery deserve honorable mention because, in addition to marching as we did, they were both severely beaten and injured.

However, there are three specific marches that stand out in my memory, which I will never forget. Two of them stand out because they were the most frightening. Again I was only 14 years old at this time, the third was the most joyful event of the movement.

1. One Scary Night at Camp Selma

Because the authorities were running out of jail space, as the movement leaders had planned, they emptied a penitentiary facility near Selma, called Camp Selma, and moved the prisoners to another nearby county that had vacant jail space. I was arrested in a march sometime in early 1965, and a bus load of us were taken to Camp Selma. We, all males, were put into an empty room with a concrete floor, and a tub of water in the center of the floor. The prisoners' bunks had been moved out of this room. We were forced to sit on the cold, hard concrete floor. For a while we sat quietly in this semi-dark room. Then all of a sudden, out of nowhere the white officers started screaming at us, like drill sergeants, calling us "niggers" and "cursing" in very intimidating voices. This was the first time I had experienced that level of vicious aggression. We had not been coached for this level of intense intimidation. The officers forced us to line-up in the corner of another room, nose-to-head, and each man, one behind the other. As I remember, the wall was long enough for about a 20 man deep line. So, a 20 man deep line, with 10 men across means there were about 200 young men, mostly high school students, who were pushed into a corner, and packed tight with little space to move, or breathe.

In addition to the racial slurs, and name calling, the last man on the end of each row was shocked with cattle prods, which forced them to push hard, and forward making the huddle tighter. We were ordered not to "take our nose off the head of the man in front", and "not to turn around and look back." The guys in back who were being prodded did a lot of hollering, and screaming that night. Several of them "fainted", I was fortunate enough to be smaller and hidden down in the middle of the pack. But I was still gasping for air, dripping with sweat, and I was horrified, not knowing what these evil men would do next. After about 20 minutes of torture and intimidation, we were put back into the big empty room. We were finally released that night after about three hours of being confined. This was a very frightening night, and the first time, I thought I might die, or be killed in the movement. But unfortunately it would not be the last.

2. Bloody Sunday – March 7, 1965

Bloody Sunday was the most infamous, and by far the most brutal of all the Selma marches. This was the march that "stunned" America, and showed the world the true depth of racial segregation and discrimination that existed in Selma and the south. Because this march was televised across the nation;

it is also the march that achieved the most significant gains for Selma and the Civil Rights Movement. In this march, at the order of Alabama Governor George Wallace, approximately 100 law enforcement officers (state troopers, county deputies, and city policemen) attacked, beat, and tear gassed 600 marchers heading from Selma to Montgomery to protest for the right to vote at the state capital. I was marching with my brother, Joe (16), and my cousin Ellis (Pee Wee) (13) *(deceased 2007, Long Beach, CA)*. Our positions were within the first 200 marchers from the front, because when the beating started and the tear gas was thrown, we had already come over the bridge, and were at ground level in front of the Tractor Company, on the north side of the bridge.

- *I Really Feared For My Life This Time*

The tear gas was the worst thing I had ever smelled! My eyes burned, I was coughing relentlessly, and felt like I was choking. As the troopers rushed the crowd, clubbing those at the front, and pushing them to the ground: John Lewis, Ms. Amelia Boynton, Hosea Williams, etc. the three of us broke rank and ran into the tractor company yard, and then down behind the building. Fortunately, no troopers followed us, and neither one of us were hit, or hurt. Somehow, while the crowd was still in pandemonium, and through the cloud of tear gas, we made our way back across the bridge. To this day, I don't remember anything else from that point. I don't remember the route we took back to the church. I don't remember if we went back to the church, or to my Aunt Etta's house in the GWC project, across the street from Brown Chapel Church. But 50 years later, March 7, 1965 still holds the record as "the most frightening day of my life. "This is the only time I can remember feeling that my death was imminent!"

From Selma to Salvation

3. Marching into Montgomery, the rally at the State Capitol

The beating of marchers at the bridge on Bloody Sunday, fueled a righteous anger and determination in Dr. Martin L. King that most of us had never seen before. He called for another march to Montgomery and he called for all Americans to "come to Selma" and march with us! The result of this national call was one of the most astounding and encouraging events that I have ever witnessed. Thousands of people came to Selma; people of all nationalities, from every city, and state, and some even came from other countries. News reporters, and camera men with tons of vehicles and equipment littered the streets around Brown Chapel Church, day in and day out. I had never seen anything like this before. For weeks during this phase of the movement, the normal population of Selma (28, 300 in 1965), swelled and increased by several thousand people. The spot light of the nation and the world was on Selma. And Dr. King, being the master strategist that he was, used this spotlight moment to further advance the Civil Rights agenda.

Many black Selma families opened their homes, and took in the newcomers who had come to town to march with us. These poor families who had only meager resources themselves, and small cramped homes, made room, and stretched their budgets; some slept on floor pallets in their own homes, gave up their beds, and fed out of town marchers for up to a month. My Aunt Etta who lived near the church in the GWC housing project provided room and board for three white priest. I remember being intrigued by their black suits and white collars. I later learned that these ministers were affiliated with the Unitarian Universalist Church. Unfortunately, one of those ministers, Rev. James Reeb, was beaten to death by a group of white men in downtown Selma, near the Silver Moon Café on

From Selma to Salvation

March 11, 1965 for being a sympathizer and a participant in the Selma Movement.

We, teen boys, became entrepreneurs, earning up to $20 per day running errands to the local stores for camera men and reporters. As a 9th grade high school student, I and many of my classmates did not attend school for the entire month of March 1965. We showed up every day at Brown Chapel Church to march or attend mass meetings. The wisdom and foresight of our parents, teachers, and the community at large to let us stay out of school to march still baffles me to this day. They told us we were making history, and what we were doing was important. But of course, we were too young to understand the full implications of their statements. In spite of the apparent danger, my mother never prohibited me from attending mass meetings and marches. She would only say: "stay with your brother." Joe was two years older.

After three failed attempts to march from Selma to Montgomery to protest voting rights for blacks, finally on March 21, 1965 a federal court order was granted to permit the march. President Lyndon B. Johnson was persuaded through multiple events to send federalized National Guard troops to protect the marchers on the 54 mile journey. This march was launched from Selma with a racially, and regionally mixed multitude of approximately 5,000 marchers; over 50% of them were out of towners, not from Selma, nor Alabama. From this point, the victory and goal of Dr. King and the Selma Movement was effectively already accomplished. However, the Voting Rights Act of 1965, prohibiting and preventing all acts of discrimination against black voting in Selma, Alabama, and the south was not signed into law until August 6, 1965, by President Lyndon Johnson.

My brother, Joe, was in the final march, and he marched the entire 54 miles to Montgomery. I don't remember why, but I was not in the first leg of the final march. However, transporters from Selma were taking people to join the March every day. On the third day of the march, I caught the transport truck and joined the marchers just inside the city limits of Montgomery at the St. Jude High School campus. A tent city had been set-up in back of the school on the athletic field. The marchers were in a very celebratory mood and I did not sense any tiredness or exhaustion in them. People were singing the traditional freedom songs: *"Ain't Gonna Let Nobody Turn Me Round," "Way Over Yonder",* and *"We Shall Overcome."*

An entertainment stage had been erected and celebrities including: Sammy Davis, Jr, Harry Belafonte, Tony Bennett, Parnell Roberts (Adam Cartwright, from the TV series – *Bonanza)* were freely mingling, greeting marchers, and performing.

On March 24, 1965, we (the marchers) left St. Jude's campus and walked the 4 miles to the Alabama State Capitol. All the way along the route standing about 10 feet apart on both sides of the streets were armed military soldiers. Most of them were white, and they were there to protect us, the marchers. On this day, I felt no fear. Also lining streets on both sides were blacks who were not in the march, but they waved and cheered us on. There were also some white people lining the streets, but none of them were celebrating; most were stone faced, and some were visibly angry.

By the time we arrived at the State Capitol, the number of marchers had risen to 25,000. From the front steps of the Capitol down Dexter Avenue, as far as the eye could see, for at least a mile, there were wall to wall people. This was an amazing site to see! I was positioned with my brother Joe, a few hundred feet from the Capitol steps off to the left side. We had a good visual position. A victory celebration rally was held on the Capitol steps. Beyond Dr. King's speech, I don't remember who else spoke, or what else was said. Honestly, I was too enamored by the crowd, and all of the excitement and movement associated with that day. I had never been in a crowd this large, nor had I ever seen this many black and white people together in unity, working for a common cause. This gathering was the most impressive event I had ever witnessed, observed, or participated in. The impact was life-changing.

But what I do remember is that it was a great day of celebration, and there was a great sense of victory in the air. I believed Dr. King's dream would come true, and I felt that we as a people were on the road to equality.

Lessons Learned

1. *It was not until decades after leaving Selma and the movement ended that I understood the value of being able to witness these young black Civil Rights leaders making history, firsthand.*

2. *The fact that they were ministers and men of courage who were beaten and died fighting for equality for African-Americans significantly impacted my life. They helped make America a "more perfect union."*

3. *In time, I grew to become immensely proud of my race, my people, and my heritage.*

4. *As I look back with a more seasoned understanding of God's grace and favor, I am so thankful, and filled with*

immense gratitude for the small place in history God has sovereignly allowed me to experience. Only He could have divinely "ordered my steps" in this way.

5. *Because of this experience, I have a uniquely different vantage point from which I view all of life. And it is from this vantage point that I find and live out my life purpose. I pray that I will faithfully finish well, as did my Civil Rights heroes.*

6. *The most important thing a boy or man can do is find his "life purpose." I think it was Dr. King who said: "A man who dies without finding his life purpose, has never truly lived."*

7. *At some point in time life and history will call upon every man to take a stand, fight for a cause, or serve a purpose greater than himself. The man who hears the call, and accepts the challenge, will inevitably find his "life purpose." The one who does not, will spend the rest of his life searching for it!*

Chapter Three

They Killed the King

The Montgomery Victory Celebration Did Not Last Long

Once the Selma to Montgomery celebration rally on the State Capitol steps ended, the logistics of getting all the marchers back to Selma began. Some volunteers were transporting people in their cars. SCLC/march organizers had leased the City of Montgomery buses to take us back to Selma. I remember getting on a bus on the evening of March 25th about 7 or 8 pm. The 45 minute drive put us back in Selma at Brown Chapel Church about 9 pm.

Ms. Viola Liuzzo Shot and Killed

When we arrived at the church, we received the bad news that one of the volunteers transporting people by car, Mrs. Viola Liuzzo, a white female mother and housewife from Detroit, had been killed by Klansmen who shot into her car with a shot gun. Riding in the car with her was one of my schoolmates, Leroy Morton (*his younger sister – Diane Morton, was in my graduating class).* This tragedy instantly sapped the celebratory feelings of the day. Fortunately, Leroy Morton was not killed, but he was slipped out of town immediately for his own safety.

They Killed the King

After we returned home from Montgomery, the turbulent atmosphere in Selma that had plagued the town for the entire month of March 1965 felt like it was waning, and my hometown was beginning to feel normal again. Many of us, students, who had been out for the marches returned to school. I remember attending a dance at the Hudson High School gym on Friday, April 5th, 1968 the day after Dr. King was killed. Before, the dance was over, we decided to march down First Avenue in protest.

The news that Dr. King had been shot in Memphis and killed was heart-wrenching. I will never forget that night, or the date. I was just two months away from my high school graduation. Shock, horror, hurt and anger spread through the gym. All of the students in the gym, without a leader or instruction, bolted out of the gym into the street, and we marched down First Avenue toward downtown. We marched and sang for a while, but we never made it downtown. By the time we reached Broad Street, the painful reality of what had happened hit us. We were just teenagers trying to process these terrible tragedies we were experiencing in Selma. The march dispersed, and we all went home seeking consolation from our parents. I would pass Brown Chapel Church on the way home, but I don't remember stopping by the church that night.

The days and weeks after Dr. King was killed are mostly a blur in my memory. I am sure there was a memorial service at Brown Chapel, and our family watched the entire funeral events unfold on TV, and there were probably chartered buses from Selma to Atlanta to the funeral service. But I don't remember attending any of those events.

Lessons Learned

1. *Every privilege, right, opportunity or benefit we have in life is because someone else made a sacrifice for us; so we should demonstrate gratitude, excel in some life endeavor, and "pay it forward."*

2. *Men who are called and destined to be liberators and reformers generally don't live to attain old age. They are considered dangerous and a threat to society while they live. They are only celebrated after their deaths, when the "powers that be" feel safe and secure again. Fortunately, the work of many liberators and reformers have societal impact long after they are gone.*

Chapter Four

Leaving Selma – Free At Last

From Selma to Salvation

The next major event in my life was the day I left Selma. On Friday, May 31, 1968, I graduated from R.B. Hudson high school and received my diploma. On Saturday, the next day, June 1st, I boarded a Greyhound Bus, left Selma, and headed to Toledo, Ohio to live with Uncle Ulysses and Aunt Essie and work for the summer.

I don't remember consciously planning such an abrupt departure from Selma, but I was a determined, goal and action-oriented person. Now that I had finished high school, I saw no need to hang around Selma. I do vividly remember concluding that, "I would never live in Selma, Alabama, or the south again, nor would I raise my children there." As soon as I made it to Ohio that summer, I began to mentally disassociate myself from Selma, the State of Alabama, and the distressing events of the Civil Rights Movement. I was embarrassed and ashamed by those events. Apparently, the humiliation of being beaten, jailed, and treated inhumane had some lingering emotional effects on me; even though I was not conscious of it at the time. I also had some hidden anger and resentment. Apparently, in my mind, I had done all I could to help change the situation. Dr. King our leader had given his all and had been assassinated. So, I was done with Selma, Civil Rights, and the South. I never remember verbalizing these thoughts, and feelings, but this was clearly my state of mind.

Traveling North

During the black migration north, from the south during the 1950's and 60's "Alabama to Detroit" was a primary route and destination for blacks seeking a better life and opportunities. At least eight of my mother's siblings had migrated to Detroit. However, Toledo was the first of what would become regular

Summer trips north. It was a metro area of 600,000 people, with a city population of about 200,000. Small in comparison to Detroit, but large in comparison to Selma, Alabama (pop. 20,000).

Aunt Essie lived on the south side, on Blum Street. It was a mostly black middle class community. There were no housing projects in the immediate vicinity. The community was probably about 30 years old, but still clean and well kept. The houses were mostly single story family homes, some two stories mixed in. Streets were paved with sidewalks, the yards had green grass. It was mostly a quiet neighborhood, and there was a nice city park, just a few blocks away. One block south was a main street, Nebraska, where I quickly learned to catch the bus downtown.

Uncle Ulysses and Aunt Essie were nice and hospitable, they made me feel welcome and at home. Because they only had one child, my cousin Gwen, in a three bedroom house, I had my own room. Ulysses drove a nice car, and they lived in a comfortable, white, wood framed house. But church was noticeably absent from their lives, and also from my life at that time. At 17 years old, I rarely had any thoughts of God, church or religion. I was enjoying and getting to know the world outside of Selma, and it felt good. I was now beginning to understand the reason behind the great black migration north that I had often heard about from relatives who traveled back home to the south on holidays and vacation.

Experiencing Integration

My first job in Toledo was with the city of Toledo, City Parks & Recreation Departmont. I worked all day with a tall, red-haired, white guy named Phil Rue. He was a student at the

University of Toledo, working a Summer job like myself. Our job was to drive throughout the city to all the parks and clean the outdoor toilets. Our mode of transportation was a green army jeep, with a City of Toledo logo, and cleaning supplies in the back. Phil was the driver, he obviously knew the city, and I was the side kick.

This was the first time either one of us had experienced working with a person of the opposite race this closely and for an extended period of time. We rode together in a jeep every day, all day, for two and a half months. During this time we talked about everything, and we got to know each other quite well. Phil was a nice guy. I never detected any hint of racism about him. He was a bit lazy, and loved white rock bands. This was my first time hearing about rock groups like: the Rolling Stones, the Doors, and Creedence Clearwater Revival. And I am certain it was his first time hearing about Motown, and the Temptations. Phil and I shared and learned from each other. We worked some, and goofed off some. One day we stopped by his home I met his mom, and saw his extensive record collection. He also showed me the University of Toledo (UT) campus where he went to college. I was impressed. UT was not a large campus, but it was a step above my Alabama A&M College campus.

I had an even more interesting, and hilarious racial integration experience that summer with the white kids we met in the parks. In those days (1968 –1970), I wore a three inch long Afro hair style. The kids were fascinated by my hair and they often asked to touch it. So, on more than one occasion that summer, I had little white fingers digging through my hair, and describing what it felt like. The kids were fun. I thoroughly enjoyed their intrigue. Without knowing it at that time, I was experiencing life and people as God meant for the human race to interact: as equals, accepting, loving, sharing and respecting one another. This was the beginning of many more racial integration experiences to come. And I enjoyed it. Working with Phil and playing with the white kids in the Toledo parks were very affirming experiences for me. The mysterious thing about it is that none of us knew it was happening at the time. I can look back and clearly see how God was setting my life up for some unique interracial encounters that would wipe away the scars, pain and anger of Selma.

Lessons Learned
---

1. We are most like God when we love and accept one another as equals, and embrace the uniqueness and differences which God has placed in each one, and everything He created.

2. Children are the best speakers and interpreters of the universal language called "love." They don't question it, judge it, or manipulate it. They just accept and give it back in return.

Tempted By the Black Nationalist Movement

When I arrived in Toledo, Ohio in the summer of 1968, one of the things that caught my attention was the Black Nationalist rhetoric of both the Black Panthers and the Black Muslim Movements. These movements were challenging the non-violent philosophy of Dr. Martin L. King and the SCLC-Civil Rights Movement. This "stand up and fight back" rhetoric was intriguing to angry young black males who felt that we would never attain justice while white racist Americans had guns, and we had none. The assassination of Dr. King, and the national outbreak of rioting, looting and burning that spread across the major cities of America made this rhetoric tempting to me. On occasion I would go down to Door Street, the black main street in Toledo to get a haircut, shop, or just hang out around the pool hall with my buddies, Sometimes, I would buy and read their newspapers. The black self-defense message seemed reasonable, but the harsh revolutionary rhetoric to "kill the pigs" (policeman) was disconcerting to me. Even though I was not involved in church at this time in my life, I still had a God consciousness and moral values about right and wrong. I had grown up in the church all of my life, and I valued and respected Dr. King and his philosophy of love and non-violence. I knew that killing of any innocent people was wrong. So, I made the decision to stand on the morals and values I had been taught by the people I respected. I stopped reading the Black Nationalist Movement papers.

For the next two summers, I returned to Toledo during the college breaks to work. I found jobs quite easily. I worked for Toledo Edison Power Company and Libby-Owens-Glass Company. The summer of my senior year, I went to Detroit, instead of Toledo, and lived with my cousins, Alma Jean and Henry. I worked at the Chrysler Mack Stamping plant. This was also the summer I bought my first car, while I was still in college. A 1964 Pontiac Tempest, it cost $750. Cousin Henry co-signed the note, my monthly car note was $62.50. I paid it off in one year.

Lessons Learned

1. *Be aware, be skeptical, and reject new information, new movements, and new people that attempt to lead you away from the values and beliefs that are biblically based; learned from the people who loved you, cared for you, and taught you before you ever knew right from wrong (2 Timothy 1:5).*

2. *Any teaching that promotes doing harm to another person, is evil, and cannot be from God, because God is good!*

3. *As a parent and a father, I learned that one of the keys to growing a boy into a man, is to insist that he learn the value of work, earning money, and paying his own way early in life.*

The Blessing of Family Made Growing Up Easier

Having a large extended, close knit, family was a blessing. There were 17 siblings in my maternal family. Those who had migrated from Alabama to the north still came home on major holidays. My maternal grandmother (*Nettie Florence Calhoun*) lived to the age of 96, and she was the primary reason why relatives from the north made the annual pilgrimage back to Alabama. They welcomed me, and other younger relatives who wanted to come north to better their lives.

Lessons Learned

1. *No man (or person) is self-made; if you have accomplished anything, if you are successful at anything, someone else helped you.*

2. *If as a young person you happen to obtain knowledge and education that your elders did not have the opportunity to do, your attitude should not be that you are better than them, instead go back to those who helped you, and help them become better.*

From Selma to Salvation

Returning to Alabama to Finish College

I left Toledo and Detroit at the end of each summer, and returned to Huntsville, Alabama in the fall to attend college at Alabama A&M College. Finishing college and earning my degree was important for several reasons: 1. it was the only way I could express thanks to my father who died in military service for making provisions for our family in his absence. 2. It was honoring to my mother who was a constant reminder of the inheritance Daddy had left, and the value of education. 3. I made an observation during the summers that I traveled north, and worked blue collars jobs. Most young blacks that I met in the north were not college bound. Factory jobs were plentiful, and they seemed content with that. I had no desire to work a factory job for a lifetime. It was hard and dirty work, and utilizing the hands were more important than using the brain. I was a good student, I enjoyed school, God had given me a brain, and I wanted a professional career; even though I was not sure what that career would be at the time.

Though Huntsville was in Alabama and the south, demographically it was different from other parts of the State. As the home of Redstone Arsenal, the U.S. Army Missile Command, and many other support industries, the city attracted a highly technological, and racially diverse workforce. It was perhaps the most progressive city in Alabama. The population (137,000 in 1970) was substantially larger than Selma's. Economically, Huntsville/Madison County, Alabama did not have a U.S. designated poverty zone. The houses and neighborhoods that we lived in off campus as students were superior to some of the houses our families lived in at home in Selma. In addition, by being away from Selma for a while, I was able to overcome some of the resentment that had built up in me during the Movement years

Chapter Five

Finding My Place in the World

My college years were an enjoyable time of life. Several of my high school classmates were also on campus: Coleman Eaton, Willie Darrington, Jackie Brown and Winona Chestnut. So, there was a "Selma crew" in the house. Coleman and I had become friends in high school, and we remained roommates for the entire three and a half years I was in college.

The Selma people I grew up with have a unique, self-perpetuating bond that I have not seen or experienced with other people, and in other places where I lived. It remains intact 47 years after we left high school. Maybe our Civil Rights experience play an unknown part, or maybe it's the fact that some us and our families have literally known each other all of our lives. For instance, Barbara Grace and I grew up in the same east Selma neighborhood, and we were in first grade together, Ms. Durant's class. How unusual is that? My friendship with Coleman has lasted for over four decades, though we spent years apart while pursuing our careers. We still play golf together in Atlanta regularly.

Our classmates still come together bi-annually for a reunion (birthday bash) in different cities, and several of us: Coleman, Reginald, Willie D, Ora, Sally, Hattie and Chellette, who live in the Atlanta/Alabama area stay connected. My Selma connection is one of those small blessings of life that I thank the Lord for, and quietly treasure in my heart. Over the years, I learned to appreciate my small town, Deep South roots even more.

At A&M mingling and interacting everyday with 1,500 of my contemporaries from all across the state of Alabama, and a few other states outside of Alabama was a great opportunity for socialization, and building lifelong relationships. Games, parties, and girls were all a part of my extra curricula activities.

But school and education was my forte. I thoroughly enjoyed the entire college life experience. Of course, the best part of my college experience besides getting a degree, was meeting and marrying my soulmate, Betty Faye Whitlow.

My college years went by fast, being the fast-tracker that I am, I graduated in three and one-half years, one semester earlier than my class in December 1971. I interviewed for a job with the Department of Defense (DOD) in a business field, procurement and contracting in the college placement office, and was hired on the spot. I don't remember being too serious about a job at the time, but I had one now, and I was required to report to work in January 1972, one month after graduation. No cap, no gown, no ceremony. All I had was a certificate of completion from the registrar's office. My official diploma would not be ready until May 1972, and I could return to campus to march in the graduation, but I did not. What I did not understand at the time is that I was hired as an overseas employee. But I would remain in the states for one year for training. Man! I was moving fast and far! And guess where they sent me for training? New Mexico!

A place I had never heard of before, a place most people had never heard of: White Sands Missile Range, Las Cruces, New Mexico. What in the world? If I had really processed and understood all of the ramifications of this job, I probably would have declined the offer. Of all the military bases the U.S. Army/Department of Defense (DOD) had, why was I sent to New Mexico? Huntsville, Alabama had excellent procurement training facilities, why couldn't I stay there, with my girl, and my home boys, while she finished up her last year of college? I

later learned that I could have requested Huntsville as a
training site. But I didn't know that at the time. I also spent
most of that first year on Temporary Duty (TDY) traveling back
East to procurement training schools, so again, why did they
send me out west?

Only God knows the answer to those kind of "why"
questions. Looking back after many years have passed, I can
see that the hand of God was orchestrating the events of my life,
but I did not recognize it at the time. As I reflect back, from
growing up in Selma, marching in the Civil Rights Movement,
to all of the life-changing events that followed, nothing about
the unfolding of my life was normal. But I was adventurous,
loved a challenge, and was afraid at times, but not enough to
quit. The thought of clinging to things that were familiar, home,
family and friends, did not linger for long. I knew there was
another world outside of Selma, and Alabama, and I wanted to
explore it.

Go West Young Man – My First Real Job

One month after graduating from college in December 1971,
I was scheduled to report to my new job in Las Cruces, New
Mexico. I spent the Christmas holidays at home with family,
said good-bye to my teary eyed fiancé, Betty Faye, packed my
1964 Pontiac Tempest with my trunk and my 12 inch black &
white TV, and headed west from Alabama to New Mexico; on a
1200 mile trip, alone, across the desert southwest. This trip
was the beginning of many first, adventuresome, and
sometimes frightening, risk-taking, life-changing decisions I
would make in the coming years. My mother was my greatest
supporter; she never objected to any worthwhile venture that
I undertook, but I later learned that her heart was gripped with
fear at times as I sat out to find my place in the world.

Lessons Learned

Don't let fear of the unknown stop you from discovering and experiencing some wonderful opportunities in life; almost everything we know today was unknown at some point in time.

I vividly remember the first day, in January 1972 that I drove into the small mostly Mexican town of Las Cruces, New Mexico. A tumble weed, exactly like the kind I had seen on TV so many times while watching western movies, rolled across the street by a moderate wind. I checked-in to the Rodeway Inn Motel, and immediately called my sponsor Mr. Sam Bone to let him know I was in town. He was gracious, and invited me to his home for dinner the same evening. I was relieved to discover that Sam Bone was a black man, from Huntsville, Alabama. He worked as an engineer at White Sands Missile Range, the same place I would be employed. Sam and his wife Alma welcomed and adopted me into their family. They lived in a beautiful, all brick home on a desert lot outside of town.

Reconnecting With My Church Roots

If you go into any city or town in America and want to find the black people, stop by the local Missionary Baptist, or AME churches and you will find them. The small Mexican city of Las Cruces had one Missionary Baptist Church, and the Bone family were members there. Of course, I being the new young, black, single man in town was invited to come. Since, I had nothing else to do, and didn't know anyone else in town I agreed to go. On the first Sunday, I met all of the 50 black people and their families that lived in town. Most of them also lived on one street in town, Paxton Street, in modest homes. A number of the young adults from the church were students at New Mexico State University (NMSU). So, the church and the college campus became my hang-out places.

I quickly became close friends with Andrew Trotter, one of the older young adults in the church. He had graduated from NMSU, was a Social Worker, and he was the best man at me and Faye's wedding. For primarily socialization purposes, I became a member at the Baptist Church (I don't remember the name of the church because I only stayed there one year). I do remember that the pastor's name was Rev. Williams. The Las Cruces black Baptist Church was very similar to my home church back in Selma. The people were friendly and affirming. I even became an usher. It was a nice social environment. But I have no memory of having any kind of spiritual awakening while attending church there.

Another Racial Integration Experience

My first housing experience in Las Cruces, New Mexico expanded my racial integration background. I shared a house with two (2) white males, Dean and Terry. Dean was a Caucasian, who worked at New Mexico State University. Terry was an older student from northern New Mexico, who was partially native American (Indian); and of course me, an African-American male from Selma, Alabama. We jokingly called ourselves the United Nations (U.N.) The three of us actually got along well, and had good times together, even though we pretty much lived separate lives. Outside of Selma, and the Civil Rights Movement, the world and people seemed to be kind, affirming and living in harmony. I was growing and developing into a citizen of the world. Much of the resentment I carried against the system of segregation in Alabama was gradually disappearing because I was encountering people who treated me as an equal.

God Shows Up and Plants a Spiritual Seed in my Life

Most people who lived in Las Cruces and worked at White Sands Missile Range made the 30 minute commute by shuttle bus. Once I got situated, I also stopped driving and began to take the shuttle bus. One day on the return trip from work back to the commuter parking lot, I sat beside a young white male. We had a pleasant conversation, toward the end of the trip he offered me a small yellow booklet to read. It was called "the Four Spiritual Laws." I graciously took the booklet and thanked him for it. I am sure I read it at some point in time, but I don't remember when, anyway nothing changed in my life at that time. Looking back, I can clearly see that this encounter was one of God's seed sowing experiences in my life, because five years later, as a Campus Crusade Lay Staff Person, I was teaching – *"Four Spiritual Laws* – evangelism class in Detroit. But let's not get too far ahead of God! He is getting ready to show-up in a big way in my life!

Lessons Learned

1. *"For I know the plans I have for you says the Lord, plans to prosper you, and not harm you, plans to give you hope and a future." (Jeremiah 29:11)*

2. *The four spiritual laws booklet says – "God loves you, and He has a wonderful plan for your life." I believe that God has a good and perfect life plan for every person. The question is "How do you get to know His plan for your life?" Read Matthew 7: 7, 8 and find out.*

From Selma to Salvation

Chapter Six

Spiritual Conversion on a Foreign Mission Field

From Selma to Salvation

In many ways the farther, I traveled away from Selma, the better life became. But honestly, I never intended to leave the U.S. at the age of 22, and actually move to a foreign country. But that's exactly what happened. I finished my first year of Procurement and Contracting training state-side, and then I was off to Yokohama, Japan.

Not Leaving Without my Soulmate

Among my family and friends who know me well, I am known as action-oriented and decisive. My Choleric temperament cannot tolerate "indecisiveness." So, as soon as I found out that I would be transferred to Japan, the following year, I phoned my fiancé, Betty Faye, back at college in Huntsville, Alabama, and told her that we had to do a quick wedding, while she finished her senior year of college. Being married was a requirement before she could be processed as a dependent to travel with me to Japan. We had been dating since her freshman year, so the wedding was inevitable, and I was not about to travel to the "Far East" without my girl. I was bold and adventurous, but not stupid. I was given a new assignment with only a six month window of time. She agreed to the quick wedding, and her family in Alabama quickly made preparations and flew her out to New Mexico.

My adopted family, the Bones, and the church members all pitched in and gave us a beautiful church wedding. Sam Bone pulled some strings and got us a beautiful Presbyterian church sanctuary, and the pastor, Rev. Nelson Wurgler, to perform the ceremony. It was beautiful, in spite of the fact that we only had three months to plan it. We honeymooned in the "Land of Enchantment", New Mexico where I was already living. My bedroom in the modest range home where I lived with my roommates, Dean and Terry was our "honeymoon suite." They came to the wedding, but stayed away from the house over the weekend to give us privacy.

Faye and I were married in March 1972, and in January 1973, we flew off to Honolulu, Hawaii, and had a super honeymoon at the U.S. government's expense. I was assigned temporary duty (TDY) at Pearl Harbor Naval Station for one month to complete a Cost and Price Analysis course. Life was good, and we were living it up until I came back to the hotel one day after class, and my new bride broke into tears, saying "I want to go home!" I was perplexed. On the one hand, my heart was breaking because "this sweet little Alabama country girl" had left home for the first time, and was half-way around the world missing her family. On the other hand, I wanted to laugh because the bad news which I did not say, was "sorry honey, you can't go home!" And within a few weeks, it would get worse because we would be traveling several more thousand miles away from Alabama to Japan. Literally on the other side of the world. I don't remember what I said or did to console her, we probably made a phone call home to her mother. But after this episode, she adjusted well, and never had another breakdown.

Once we arrived in Japan, Faye moved into a good career because her degree was in English, and she became a teacher at a Catholic school, St. Maurs International School. This was an English speaking school where many of the diplomats, ambassadors, and international business people children attended school. The Japanese employment system paid employees bonuses several times each year. So, Faye's job doubled our income, but we didn't live out of her salary. We banked 100% of it. I got the idea from reading a financial investment magazine, and we practiced it the entire time we lived in Japan. My government income and housing allowance were sufficient. So, we began building a financial nest egg, and we sent money back home to Alabama each month to help our mothers. Economic empowerment was a part of Dr. King's "dream" for black America. We were now beginning to live that dream. In just five years, after leaving Selma, my economic status had improved drastically, our combined salaries, and household income placed us solidly in the American middle class. Now I was beginning to understand and appreciate: 1. the value of education. 2. the importance of what we did in Selma, protesting, marching and going to jail for equal rights. 3. the sacrifices our parents and older African-Americans had made in order for us to be in this position. It would be a while longer before I understood the grace and favor of God that was also operating in my life at that time.

Lessons Learned

1. *"But if a widow has children or grandchildren, these should learn first of all to put their religion into practice by caring for their own family and so repaying their parents and grandparents, for this is pleasing to God."*

2. *One of the great lessons I learned, accidentally by the way, was the blessing of giving back money to help my mother. I practiced this principle as long as my mother was living, and today, I am still reaping benefits in ways that I cannot even calculate.*

3. *God's greatest blessings in my life are not things, but people. By the grace of God, I have always be surrounded by a village of good people.*

From Selma to Salvation

His Grace and Mercy Kept Drawing me Back to the Church

I was a civilian U.S. Army employee, and enlisted military personnel had the first option for housing on-base. Therefore, we had to seek housing off base in the Yokohama community, which proved to be a wonderful culture experience. Nevertheless, we still had access to government issued furniture. The housing office also had a list of private renters in the community that were approved for leasing properties to U.S. civilian personnel living off-base. We found a quaint little two bedroom house in Negishi Heights. Our landlord was Mr. Lin. I remember him as a kind, gentle, and small man who always wore a smile. His polite demeanor typified the polite, courteous Japanese culture.

The weather in Yokohama, Japan was mild on the day in March 1973, when we followed a military truck home with our government issued furniture. Most of the street signs we passed along the way were written in Japanese Kanji, so I could not read them. But I do remember passing and reading one sign, in particular, it read: "Yokohama International Baptist Church." I remember saying to Faye, "once we move in, let's come back and check out this church." It was located only a short drive up the hill from our house. I was not sensing a spiritual hunger in my life, but I thought attending church would be a nice thing to do. After all, that is the way I was raised. But I now know that the Spirit of God was still drawing me to Himself. Sure enough within a week or two after we moved into our house, we got up one Sunday morning and went back to the church on the hill. We had already purchased a small used car. Cars were plentiful and cheap because so many military personnel transferred in and out so frequently. We only paid $500 for our ten year old Hino Contessa, it was good dependable transportation.

I wasn't sure what to expect when Faye and I got to the new church, we knew it would not be black Baptist or AME. So we decided to go in and see what happened. To our surprise, no one seemed to notice the obvious, we were black. If they did, it didn't show. Everybody welcomed us in and greeted us. Just like people had done at the black churches back home. Even, though Yokohama, Japan was a U.S. military base city, we saw no other blacks in the church. The congregation size was about 125. The people groups included: military families, Southern Baptist missionaries *(this church was a Southern Baptist missions church plant),* some Japanese youth, U.S. businessmen, and me and Faye, a black military civilian couple.

Prior to our spiritual conversion, we attended the base NCO Club on a few occasions, we found lots of African-Americans there on the dance floor, and at the bar. But to be fair, there was probably an on-base church service where more blacks attended church, since on-base was where most enlisted military personnel lived. However, I never felt lead to inquire or search for an on-base black worship experience. As I grew older and more self-assured, I discovered that "being the only one" did not bother me. My purpose for being in a place or situation mattered more than, "how many other blacks were there."

Attending Yokohama International Baptist Church (YIBC) proved to be a growing and rewarding experience. We were made to feel welcome, so, we went back again. The style of preaching was another attractive element of the worship service. The pastor actually opened the Bible, read the Scriptures and taught the Word. I had never heard or seen that preaching style before. I understood, and could relate to everything he said. With all due respect to the black church tradition, there was no "whooping and hollering", no

From Selma to Salvation

"sweating," "stomping" or "yelling." People brought their Bibles to church, and read along with the preacher. This was a refreshing, and welcome experience for me. The preaching style stimulated me more intellectually, than emotionally, and included some "how to" instructions.

Lessons Learned

The Goodness of God and His Kindness is intended to lead us to repentance (Romans 2:4 AMP).

My only conclusion after four decades of being consistently involved in church work is that it was my divine destiny. Apparently, the short five year hiatus I took away from church during my college years was never meant to be permanent. In reflection, I was probably seeking and needed more knowledge about salvation. I needed a reason to continue attending church beyond my childhood and family heritage.

Lesson Learned

1. *In Ecclesiastes 3:1,2,11,12 – Solomon writes: "to everything there is a season, and a time to every purpose under the heaven...a time to be born, and a time to die...He has made everything beautiful in its time...there is nothing better than for people to be and do good while they live.*

2. *I have observed many people in life who spend their lives waiting for the right time to "live." The right time to live is now! I learned this valuable lesson because I lost so many loved ones early in my life.*

3. *I purpose to live every day to its fullest; within the confines of wisdom and common sense. I purpose to love and serve the people God has called me to love and serve today. I purpose to live out God's revealed will for my life every day to the best of my ability. If I live this way, and if tomorrow does not come, I will have lived a purposeful life, and hopefully I will have finished well!*

Seeds of Racism Raised its Ugly Head Even in the Church

For the eighteen months that we were in Japan, Yokohama International Baptist (YIBC) became our church home. We became members. I was assigned to teach a boys Sunday School class of 6 to 8 – 10 to 12 year old boys (white, Asian, & oriental, none were black). I enjoyed the experience, and I got to know the boys and their parents on a first name basis. During my tenure at YIBC very few other blacks came to the church. I remember one or two families visiting, but none besides me and Faye ever stayed.

But even in the Far East, even in the church, racism raised its ugly head in my life again. One Sunday, a missionary preacher named Rev. Dudley from Texas was preaching. He was a heavy set, medium height, red-faced man. He preached regularly while YIBC was going through a pastoral search. During this particular sermon, while using a sermon illustration to accent a point, Rev. Dudley pointed me out in the congregation, and said: "as only your people can do!" I assumed he was referring to a Negro spiritual. But I was shocked. Faye was not feeling well and stayed home from church that Sunday. When I got home, I told her what had happened and how offended I was. Next, I called Jim Almond, one of the deacons of the church and expressed my offense. Jim immediately identified with me, and he apologized. He said,

From Selma to Salvation

"Junnus the minute he singled you out, I felt embarrassed, and I felt a shock of embarrassment go through the entire congregation." I cried on the phone with Jim that day because this experience brought back some of the painful memories of Selma, that I thought I had left behind. But the bold activist in me quickly came to the surface, and I told Jim that I wanted to meet with the deacons and Rev. Dudley at the church. He arranged for the meeting that same day at the 6 pm evening service.

Remember I was only 23 years old at the time, these men were all in their 40's, and Rev. Dudley could have been as old as 50 years old. We met in the church office. Jim setup the meeting, and I told Rev. Dudley that I was offended by his sermon illustration, and finger pointing during the morning service. I had been in church most of my life, but never saw a preacher do that. I asked if it were possible for him to do a sermon, and an illustration without singling out anyone in the congregation, especially in an embarrassing way. Rev. Dudley was obviously embarrassed by his behavior, he offered an apology to me, and he made a commitment to change the way he preached from that moment forward. I was not even a minister at that time, but the spirit of God brought about a powerful moment of reconciliation in that church office that Sunday evening. We all embraced and parted in love.

From that time on, Rev. Dudley and I greeted and embraced each time he came to YIBC. My guess is: 1. this was the first time an older white southern Baptist missionary preacher had ever been confronted by a black man, and 2. most other black people who encountered that experience would have simply left the church offended, never returned, and concluded that the church and the white people who claimed to know God are racist. But it never occurred to me to leave the church; and I did not conclude that the church members, or Rev. Dudley were racist. This was not the first time that I heard Rev. Dudley preach, and I am sure it was not his first time seeing me in the congregation, there were only two blacks in the church. In a strange way, I think he was actually trying to give me a compliment by referring to the unique gifts of blacks who sing Negro spirituals. However, at the time, I didn't see being singled out as the only black person in a church congregation as complimentary.

I had worshipped with these people for 18 months, and I knew them, I also knew some of their children. Instead of making a racist charge against the church or the preacher, what came natural to me was to confront the issue, and give Rev. Dudley an opportunity to apologize and repent if necessary. Of course, I had no Bible or church training in spiritual restoration at that time. But maybe I was getting a preview of what God's future will for me might be.

Lessons Learned

Whenever you find yourself in an unfamiliar place, or uncomfortable situation, before you leave to seek a more familiar environment ask God to show you your purpose for being there. There are some things in life that only "you" may be called to do, or only you are supposed to see or experience. Others may not be called in that same way. If you don't do what is revealed to you as your role, it may not get done, and people may suffer unnecessarily because you did not have the courage or faith to do what needed to be done.

From Selma to Salvation

I Finally Met Jesus! Now the Church, God, and the Bible Finally Made Sense

In March 1973, Yokohama International Church (YIBC) held their annual revival. This was a weeklong event with church services being held every night. Rev. Roy Edgemon a pastor for Tokyo was the guest evangelist for the week. I don't remember what his sermon topics were on the other nights, nor do I remember how many nights I went to church during the revival. But I do vividly remember what his sermon topic and Bible text was on the night of my spiritual conversion. His topic was the "Three (3) Kind of Men", the natural man, the carnal man, and the spiritual man. The Bible text was 1 Corinthians 2: 14, 15; 3: 1-3. He clearly defined and explained the difference between these three kinds of men.

The Spiritual Man was obviously the righteous man, the one who was most pleasing and useful to God. I sensed an emotional stirring in my heart, I wanted to be a spiritual man. But I didn't know how, I didn't know what to do. At the end of his sermon, Pastor Edgemon answered my thought question. It seemed as if "he knew exactly what I was thinking." He gave the congregation an invitation to "come forward." for prayer, for salvation, or for spiritual restoration or recommitment. I had never heard or seen this done in church before. Several people got up from their seats and went forward.

I had a desire to go forward, and pray for salvation, but I was afraid. I vaguely remember elbowing Faye and whispering to her that we needed to go forward. To my relief, she was afraid too. At that very moment, again it seemed as if Pastor Edgemon, or God was reading my mind, and eliminating all my excuses for not accepting Christ that night. So the Preacher said, if anyone here is afraid to come forward, you can say this same prayer at home, and God will still save you. Whew! I was relieved, I had a way out of going down front.

I Surrendered My Life to Christ in a Little House in Negishi Heights

As soon as we got home from church that night, Faye and I went into the bedroom. We looked at each other, and we kneeled down beside our bed and repeated the prayer of salvation that Pastor Edgemon had taught us:

"Lord Jesus, I believe that you are the Son of God; thank you for dying on the cross for my sins; please forgive me for all my sins, save me, and give me eternal life."

The next night we went back to church again. At invitation time, Pastor Edgemon asked if anyone had prayed and accepted Christ at home to come up and share it with him. This night, we were not afraid. We walked up and shared with him our decision to accept Christ. He congratulated us, and prayed with us.

After that night in March 1973, I felt a new sense of joy, peace and thirst for the Word of God in my life. I bought a new Living Bible and began to read it regularly. We stayed at YIBC and continued to worship and serve in the church for fifteen months until we came back home to the U.S. in June 1974. Our normal tour of duty in Japan was scheduled for three years, but due to a U.S. Army RIF (reduction in forces), we were transferred back to the states 18 months early.

My life was going very well, and I was content. Really, I was living the life of my dreams. But I do believe, and now know that the Spirit of God was overseeing, leading and directing my movements. I believe it was the quiet inner spirit of God directing me to this church, at this place, and at this time in my life. Why? What was it that God wanted me to see and experience at YIBC, that I could not have seen or experienced in the states? Well, looking back, here are some of my thoughts on that question:

- I believe God wanted me to see, and hear the salvation message in a way that I could understand it, and in the way that I would later be called to preach it (expository Bible preaching).

- I believe God wanted me to see the Church of Jesus in operation in its larger context; on a foreign mission field. So, that as a church planter I would have a world-view of the church, not just a black, white, or USA view of the Church.

- I believe that God graciously allowed Faye and I to experience an accelerated season of love, prosperity, and world travel that would be short-lived. We lived a richer, fuller, and a more abundant life in our 4 years and 9 months of marriage, than many people do during a long-term marriage.

My salvation experience reminds me of the story of Philip and the Ethiopian eunuch in Acts 8:26-40. God dispatched Philip on a special missionary journey out into the desert to an Ethiopian eunuch who was sitting in his chariot reading the Bible without understanding. "Then Philip began with that very passage of Scripture and told him the good news about Jesus...the Spirit of the Lord suddenly took Philip away, and the eunuch did not see him again, but went on his way rejoicing."

From Selma to Salvation

After years of thinking through the questions listed above, my conclusion is that God sovereignly planned and allowed all of the events in my life to line-up for one purpose. So, that I would get to Yokohama International Baptist Church in Japan, hear Pastor Roy Edgemon's message, and accept Jesus Christ as my Savior and Lord. In my story, I was the Ethiopian eunuch, and Pastor Roy is Philip. After that night in March 1973, I quickly left Japan, because my tour of duty was cut short, and I never saw Pastor Roy again for 41 years. How amazing are the ways of God?

This story of Philip and the Ethiopian reveals some other interesting aspects of God's character:

1. *The salvation of this one man was so important to God that He commanded the Spirit to miraculously transport an evangelist to a remote location to give him understanding, and lead him to Christ.*

2. *God intended for the Gospel and salvation to be universal and spread among all people. There are no unimportant people to God.*

Lessons Learned

1. *There are no accidents, incidents or mishaps in God's plans; He sees the end of everything from the beginning.*

2. *Each place, person, situation is divinely chosen and used to get us operating in God's divine will and redemptive purpose and plan for our lives.*

3. *God's plan is always broader than our job or career, it always includes a redemptive and kingdom purpose that the natural man cannot see.*

4. *It takes a spiritual man looking beyond natural events to see God's hand at work.*

From Selma to Salvation

Chapter Seven

Back In The USA
Detroit – A Spiritual Boot Camp in the Hood

From Selma to Salvation

"My ways are not your ways says the Lord. As high are the heavens are above the earth, so are my ways above your ways, and my thoughts above your thoughts" (Isaiah 59)

People often miss the will of God for their lives because the visible part, that which they can see does not meet their expectations. But those who walk by faith, and follow the revealed will of God will always be enriched. From a White Southern Baptist Church in Japan to an Inner City Rescue Mission in Detroit. Beginning with my unique conversion experience in Japan, my spiritual journey continued to be different, diverse, and at times confusing, but life enriching.

When our missionary friends at Yokohama International Church, Frank and Evelyn Cole heard that we were leaving and returning stateside to Warren, Michigan, they referred us to a local pastor in the area named Haman Cross. However, for reasons unknown, I did not contact Pastor Cross immediately. Instead, we begin visiting some traditional black Baptist churches in the Detroit metro area. Unfortunately, by this time my church appetite had changed. The traditional brand of church no longer satisfied my spiritual need. So, in frustration, I stopped attending church again. All the while, I had forgotten the referral Frank Cole had given me to visit Pastor Cross.

Lessons Learned

1. "No one pours new wine into old wineskins. Otherwise, the new wine will burst the skins; the wine will run out and the wineskins will be ruined."

2. After having a new spiritual experience, I mistakenly tried to go back into the same old form of church in which I had grown up in Selma. It did not work for me.

3. I needed a new and different kind of church to match the new experience I had.

4. Some people love their culture and their people more than they love God. They sometimes will remain in a spiritually dead place for a lifetime, and wonder why they have never had a new spiritual encounter with God.

In my frustration, God did not abandon me. He continued to show up in almost miraculously ways. Within a few months after Faye and I returned from Japan, the Coles also came home on furlough to Royal Oak, Michigan. Frank called and asked how we were doing, I told him not so good, we were having a problem finding a good church to attend. By that, I meant "a Bible teaching" church, where the sermon was more teaching, that loud, unclear preaching. A few days later, he invited us to dinner at their home, and also invited us to travel down to Detroit, where he would be teaching a weekday Bible study at Pastor Cross' church. We agreed to go. Our apartment was located in Madison Heights, just a few minutes north of Royal Oak off I-75, after dinner we rode with Frank and Evelyn for the 20 minute drive down to the city.

As we drove up to the building, it was not a church at all. Instead, it was a one story, old brick building. The name on the front of the building read: Detroit's Afro-American Mission, it was located on Clay Street on the eastside of the city, near downtown. There was a large metal gate guarding the front door, and the building was located in the heart of the inner city. To my surprise, I knew the area, because during the summer of

From Selma to Salvation

1971 I had lived in the same neighborhood on east Bethune Street with my cousins Henry and Alma, while I held down a summer job a Chrysler Mack Stamping Plant.

Because of my previous history in Detroit, I was not frightened by the neighborhood, but I was very curious about this "church that did not look like a church." Since I had not seen an inner city rescue mission before, I had no idea what to call it. But we were guests of the Coles, there to meet the Cross Family, so we followed protocol. Once inside, they showed us around, but I was still unimpressed. There were boxes of clothes in one room, a kitchen, a dining/eating area, two classrooms, and a sanctuary/worship area, some areas were also unfinished. It was a small facility, with about 2,000 sq. ft. of space. We met Pastor Cross, and his wife Malettor. Sitting around the table, there may have been 10-12 other people, a mixture of adults and young adults.

After all the introductions and when the tour ended, we sat in a classroom, and Frank began to teach the Bible lesson. It was good and refreshing. I had not participated in a Bible study since leaving Japan. I left the Mission that evening with no real intentions of coming back, and I definitely never thought it would become our next church home. But that is exactly what happened! Detroit's Afro-American Mission became our new church home. In spite of the fact that it was not a church, in the traditional since. At this time, Faye and I were middle class, college educated, young adults, and working professional jobs, living in the suburbs, and driving a new sports car. The mission regular members were mostly young inner city kids, a few low income adult couples, and some young adult ladies with kids. To say the least, Faye and I were a demographic mismatch at the Mission. But by this time in my life and spiritual journey, I had grown accustomed to doing things in "non-traditional ways." Just as I had walked into a white Southern Baptist Mission Church in Japan, now I was becoming a member of a black inner city rescue mission church in Detroit.

Lessons Learned

1. *If you truly follow God's plan and will for your life, you will find yourself in some unique and unfamiliar places, with unfamiliar people. But it will usually be a place of blessings.*

2. *In order to find God's will for your life, you will have to learn to follow the leading of the Holy Spirit, and not follow the crowd.*

3. *However, if God is in the place and with the people, three thing will always be apparent and consistent: (a) The teaching of the Word, (b) the commitment to Jesus Christ as Savior and Lord, and (c) submission to the power of the Holy Spirit.*

I believed then, and I know now that the Mission was the right place for Faye and I to be at that time in our spiritual journey. It was the place that God had designated for us to receive spiritual mentoring and training for ministry. There were several impressive things at the Mission, the facility not being one of them, which convinced me to stay: 1. Pastor Cross, Sister Cross, and their son Haman were good Bible teachers. 2. For the first time, I met young, African - American ministers like Haman Cross and Ron Ballard who were Bible college trained, and did not display the persona of being preachers. 3. Haman was a Campus Crusade for Christ staff person, and I was exposed new opportunities to receive excellent lay training in evangelism and discipleship.

During my four year stay at the Mission from 1975 to 1978, I participated in various types of Christian outreach and evangelism training activities: four (4) spiritual laws workshops, discipleship training seminars and Bible conferences. We traveled to different cities (Chicago, Atlantic City, Atlanta, Dallas, etc.) and college campuses (Spring Arbor, University of Detroit) each year for week long conferences. The Bill Gothard Institute in Basic Youth Conflicts (IBYC) was another valuable training conference I attend during those days.

At these events, I begin to meet other black evangelical ministers: Tom Skinner, Crawford Loritts, Chuck Singleton, E.V. Hill, Melvin Upchurch, Tony Evans, etc. These men were all full-time ministers, biblically trained, and they preached and taught the Word of God with clarity and life-style application for better Christian living; just like I had been hearing in Japan for the past 18 months. During the annual conferences, we always conducted evangelistic outreach events in city parks, or neighborhoods and shared Christ, using the Four Spiritual Laws booklets. We guided people through the steps of "how to accept Christ" as Savior and Lord. This type of ministry was far beyond just church on Sunday. We were actually following the Lord's command to "go into the world, and make disciples." (Matthew 28:18-20).

Each year, I was having the experience of actually "leading someone to Christ." I recalled sitting on the curb one day with a young black man while we were having a summer block party in Detroit. Once I finished sharing the Four Spiritual Laws with him, and asked him if he wanted to pray the sinner's prayer to receive Christ, his comment was: "you mean right here?" I said "yes, right here!" This young black male associated "praying to God with being in church." The unspoken question, and assumed religious tradition was: "How could anyone possibly make a connection with God sitting on a street curb?" "We only talk to God in church." I had grown up in Selma with a similar religious tradition. In Detroit with the Campus Crusade urban outreach programs, I was breaking away from that tradition, and learning that the Gospel of Christ was not confined to the four walls of a church.

Before long, I was a teaching Bible classes and leading young adult urban mission trips. I now had a vision for ministry, and a willingness to serve. If the Lord ever called me into ministry I now knew exactly what kind of minister I wanted to be. I did not want a ministry that confined me within the four walls of a church office all day, and where I would only preach to the same people every Sunday. I felt called to be out in the marketplace moving and mingling with people during their normal daily lives, and sharing the Gospel with them in their daily environments. Sometimes, by simply giving them a small booklet called the Four Spiritual Laws to read. I was beginning to understand that Christian living and sharing the Gospel were supposed to be daily lifestyle activities.

My Family Became My First Mission Field

It was also during this time (1975 –76), that I began to sense a burden to share the Gospel with my family members. My maternal family consisted of 17 siblings. Half of them had migrated to Detroit, and the other half still lived in Alabama. They were all traditional church goers, who had great respect for God, the church and for me, as the emerging spiritual leader in the family. In addition, we were a close-knit family that loved and supported each other. It didn't matter whether we lived north or south, the family still remained intact. My family connection was another one of the inherited blessings of my life.

I started a Bible study on eastside Detroit at my Aunt Lizzy's home, 6 to 8 relatives came weekly. On holidays and vacations, when I traveled back to Alabama, I carried Four Spiritual Laws booklets, Campus Crusade transferable concepts discipleship booklets, and Christian movies (*A Thief in the Night).* I used a borrowed movie projector from the Mission. I invited relatives to my mother's home and showed the movie, and praise God! They came! Next, I made house-to-house appointments, and stopped by different relatives home to share the Four Spiritual Laws booklet, and I lead several of them to accept Christ as Savior. One of the men was Lecester Strong, my brother-in-law, who eventually became the first Pastor of Selma Community Bible Church.

As people who were historically members of the traditional Missionary Baptist Church, I am sure my family members found my out of church approach to teaching the Bible and sharing the Gospel in homes to be quite strange. But they all came, and listened intently to whatever I was saying or sharing. They gave me the utmost respect; and they still do to this day. I realize that this kind of access to share the Gospel within one's family not always the norm. So, I thank the Lord for the access He gave me to my family. The foundation for Selma Community Bible Church was being laid ten years before, I started the church, but God had not shown me the full vision then.

To the best of my knowledge, there were two driving forces for aggressive ministry to my family: 1. I had grown up in the same traditional Baptist churches that they were members of, but I never came to an understanding of "how to be truly saved" in that setting, and I did not know any other family members who had been saved. 2. through my Campus Crusade lay training, I had learned that obedience to the Great Commission (Matthew 28:18-20 – "...go into all the world and make disciples) applied to all Christians, it was Christ's last commandment to us, and I was just obeying what the Lord commanded us to do, in the best way I knew how.

But, I was blessed in this respect: 1. I had a good reputation in my family, and I had set a precedence of success educationally and economically. I was the first person in my maternal family to graduate from college. 2. Even though I have achieved success, in their eyes, I had never strayed away from God or the Church (at least not for long, I don't think they held the college years hiatus against me) 3. Thirdly, I always demonstrated love for them; whenever I came around, I was generous with my time, and my money. I genuinely enjoyed being with my family. 4. I never condemned those who were outside of the church as "sinners." I treat them all equally. I didn't drink and party with them, but I did not condemn them for doing it.

How to interact with non-Christians, or people who do not attend church without condemning them, was one of the most important evangelistic strategies I learned through the Crusade training and the Mission outreach programs. This was one of the unknown advantages of attending church at an inner city rescue mission. They were required to serve all kinds of people, most of them poor and needy. There were no padded, hardwood pews, or plush carpeted floors in our mission church. Being trained as a new Christian in this kind of environment prepared me to deal with a variety of people in my later pastoral ministries. The Mission environment also helped shape "the holistic ministry" philosophy that I hold to this day. Personally, I believe that it is literally and biblically wrong to preach to poor people without offering them some kind of social services. Ministries that focus only on people's spiritual needs, and ignore their physical, mental, or emotional needs are incomplete. I believe this what Jesus Christ modeled, and I think our contemporary churches would reach more people for Christ is they returned to "holistic models" of ministry.

As strange as it may sound, in those days, I never aspired to be a minister or preacher; nor was I ever pressured to do so by my family, my pastor, or my minister associates in Detroit. But honestly, I think they all noticed the call of God on my life for ministry long before I acknowledged it. They noticed that my zeal for evangelism and winning people to Christ was natural and unusual. After a few years of being around the Mission and doing ministry work, Pastor Cross simply called me in his office one day and said "I am going to give you a licensed to preach," and I said ok. That was it.

Chapter Eight

MY GREATEST TEST OF FAITH

From Selma to Salvation

Lord, How Do I Continue Without My Soulmate?

I met Betty Faye Whitlow during her freshmen year at Alabama A&M College at a student dance in the gym. She was a cute, petite country girl from Camp Hill, Alabama with a big smile and bow legs. From the first time we met, she stole my heart. My play boy philosophy among the guys on campus up till that time had been, "man, I am not marrying nobody's daughter!" Well needless to say, that philosophy changed abruptly when I started dating Faye. I bought her an engagement ring for Christmas of my junior year in college. I have always been the kind of person who moves fast, and make quick decisions once I decide what I want, or want to do. Making the decision to marry Faye was no exception.

By 1976, we had been together for eight years, and married for five years. From my sophomore year in college, Faye had been my soulmate and companion through every phase of my fast paced life; even though at times it was uncomfortable for her. But she never flinched, nor objected. She loved me and believed in me with all of heart, and I knew that! And from that night in March 1973, in Japan when we both kneeled down beside our bed and jointly invited Jesus Christ to be our Savior and Lord, she never waned in her faith!

She believed in me, but she also trusted God. During all of the inner city mission work we did in Detroit, and the youth conferences we attended across the U.S. each summer, the Campus Crusade training, she was right there. And I vividly remember us team teaching our first Four Spiritual Laws training session with students at the University of Detroit. She was a natural; everybody loved her; life was good. We were living our dream, serving the Lord, and tentative planning to start a family soon. Life could not get much better. But I never expected our lives to suddenly get worse.

One day in early 1975, while we living in Madison Heights, Michigan (suburban Detroit), she made an appointment to visit her gynecologist for an annual physical. He noticed a small cyst on her neck and asked her how long it had been there? Then the doctor decided to biopsy the cyst. Once she told me about the cyst, I remember noticing that it was there while we were still in Japan, but it seemed small and insignificant. After the biopsy, I received a call from her doctor at my office in Warren, Michigan about a week later. He told me the worse news I have ever heard in my life. He said that the biopsy was malignant, and it showed that Faye had Hodgkin's disease. It is a type of cancer that affects the lymph node system, and destroys white blood cells.

The doctor made an appointment for her to come in and see Dr. Freeman Wilner, an oncologist. I was literally devastated. I left my desk, walked to the hallway behind my office, went into a phone booth and called my mother in Alabama. I told her the bad news. I wept bitterly that day. I had faith in God, but something in my spirit told me that this diagnosis would not end well.

Now for the most difficult part. How do I tell Faye this terrible news? How do you tell a 24 year old vibrant, beautiful, seemingly healthy person, someone that you love with all of your heart, that she has cancer, and she might die soon? I couldn't do it! So, I simply told her that the doctor's office had called and they wanted us to come in to discuss her biopsy report. I don't remember if she asked me for any details, but if she did, I played it off. We arrived at Dr. Wilner's office at Beaumont Hospital in Royal Oak, Michigan. He greeted us and began to describe an aggressive, comprehensive treatment plan for Faye. She stared at me! I stared at the doctor! Then, I dropped my head and told him that she didn't know about her diagnosis. Dr. Wilner stopped talking about the treatment plan, and told Faye about her diagnosis.

I remember him saying that the disease had already reached stage 2 or 3; stage 4 is terminal. He spent some time educating us about Hodgkin's disease. She was just as devastated as I had been. She broke down into tears. Oh, my God what is happening here? Why is this happening to us? There are no words to describe how brokenhearted we were. How can the lives of two young adults, with so much promise, so much love for one another, so committed to serving God and loving others be torn apart by such an evil disease as cancer?

For us, the next two years were a life draining survival course. Faye went into Dr. Wilner's aggressive surgery, chemotherapy-radiation treatment program. Fortunately, by God's sovereign design Faye's mother, Annie Tinsley, through a set of unusual circumstances had already moved from Alabama to Michigan to live with us. Her presence proved to be a major source of comfort and blessing for us. Our Christian family at the Mission offered major support, as well as my tribe of maternal relatives that lived in Detroit. Faye was receiving great medical care; everything humanly possible was being done to restore her health. But God sovereignly chose not to work a miracle of healing in her case. On December 12, 1976 Faye died at the young age of 25 years old. Our Christian family from the Mission in Detroit and my maternal family from Selma converged with Faye's family in Camp Hill, Alabama to eulogize her. This was a sad time in my life, I was a broken man. I had suffered a major loss. I still had faith in God, but He seemed so distance during this time; I did not become angry with God.

Neither was I consumed with emotional "why" questions. I was mostly consumed with "what's next?" "What do I do with my life now?"

Thank God, we didn't have any children. So I did not have the added pressure of having to console motherless children. The one questionable thought I had about Faye's death was: she was the kindest, sweetest, most vivacious person I had ever known. She was so full of life. She always had a positive effect on people through her personality, her smile, without ever saying a word. She never gossiped or slandered anyone. She made me a better person. Because she exuded so much life, it only seemed fair that God would spare her of this horrible disease that destroyed her body.

Why couldn't he take me instead? I would have died for her! In my opinion she deserved life much more than I did. But God was our God, and He had the sovereign right to have the last word. Faye would have agreed with that, so I must also! I was confident of the fact that according to the Scriptures, I would see her in heaven. But for now, I must finish my course, and complete the work that God has called me to do. In my mind, I could have been a much better man, and minister with her by my side, than without her, but apparently God did not agree with my assessment, otherwise she would have lived.

Lessons Learned

After 37 years of ministry, I still do not understand some of the ways of God. "Why would He take away one excellent wife through what I would call a premature death, and then give me another one just as good two years later?" My answer is: "I don't know!" The best answer I have ever found to this question is written in the Bible in the following passage:

81

"The Lord our God has secrets known to no one. We are not accountable for them, but we and our children are accountable forever for all that he has revealed to us, so that we may obey all the terms of these instructions." (Deuteronomy 29:29-NLT)

1. *Unfortunately, many Christians and even ministers of God can get stuck, and stop at this point in their lives. They cannot move pass a significant hurt, loss, accident, injury, or change in their lives. They cannot get pass the "Why" question! Here are some insights that that may help: (a) Leave the "why" questions to God. (b) Give yourself time to heal. (c) Pray and ask Him for the strength, faith, and courage to "see His purpose in your pain", which usually includes a "message" and "maturity." (d) move forward with your life, as best you can; slowly at first, and then pick up the pace. (e) Trust and believe that "God is good, and what He does is goodness." (f) Use your loss to help others gain.*

2. *(g) Believe that your suffering or your loved one's suffering serves a much higher eternal purpose than what you can see, feel or understand now, at the point of your pain. (h) This is the most important point! Continue to trust God, follow Him, be obedient to His Word, attend church, and stay connected to family and friends, regardless of how feel!*

3. *Express your feelings! You are human, so go ahead, and release your human emotions; in safe places, with safe people, and in safe ways. Remember, that even Jesus, the Son of God cried out in pain on the cross: "My God, My God, why have you forsaken me? But whatever you do "keep*

walking by faith!" Don't give up or give in! To depression, anger, and isolation! Then one day, in time, you will discover that there is a tremendous blessing "on the other side of your pain!" You may never be able to explain it! You may never understand it! And if given a choice, you would have never chosen this loss or pain! Whenever your restoration comes, and you can live again, just accept the blessing, and tell others about how great "God" is!

4. *I have found hope in Scriptures like: 1 Peter 5:10*

"After you have suffered a little while, the God of all grace, who called to His eternal glory in Christ, will Himself perfect, confirm, strengthen and establish you."

This verse reminds us that at some point in time, all of us will suffer. But God promise us that He will place boundaries on our suffering, and it will end.

5. *Some good books that helped me through periods of repetitive grief are:* "Don't Waste Your Sorrows," Paul E. Billheimer, Christian Literature Crusade, 1977, "Grieving the Loss of Someone You Love"-Daily Meditations, Raymond Mitsch & Lynn Brookside, Regal Book/Gospel Light, 1993, "Reflections of A Grieving Spouse", H. Norman Wright, Harvest House Publishers, 2009.

Walking Away from Success to Serve God

For the next year (1977), after Faye's death, I continued to work my civil service procurement job at the U.S. Tank-Automotive Command in Warren, Michigan, and I also maintained my Christian ministry and connection with my church family at the Mission in Detroit. I began to do some speaking at the mission, and some traveling with Pastor Cross to supporting churches in Michigan and Canada.

Without anyone actually saying it, I was being groomed for ministry. But all along, I had been nurturing a secret desire to attend Bible college and serve in Christian ministry at some point in time, Faye's death brought that ministry desire more clearly into focus. My spiritual mentor, Haman Cross, Jr stayed in close touch with me during this year. He was a consoling friend, and he gave me some invaluable advice about ministry options. After consulting with my mother to insure that she and the family would be alright financially if I resigned my job and enrolled full-time into Bible College.

I finally decided to leave my secular career and pursue full time ministry. In the African-American Baptist church circles where I grew up in the south, it was unheard of for a young college educated man to leave a professional career to pursue full-time ministry. So, there were questions and skepticism among some family members and friends when I announced that I was resigning my job. This reaction was understandable, when you consider that most small black churches could not afford to pay a pastor's full-time salary. In most cases the pastor was only paid a stipend of $100 to a few hundred dollars per Sunday.

Entering Seminary - 1978

I applied for admission to Grand Rapids Baptist Seminary. This was only two and a half hours from Detroit, so I could still remain in touch with both my maternal and Christian families. I am not sure if the Lord and Satan were having a contest about my faith during this time, as was the case in Job's life, but the testing was not over yet. I had one more major hurdle to jump even after losing Faye. Just prior to giving my resignation to the U.S. Army at the Warren Procurement Agency, I received an unexpected and very attractive job offer. The job recruiting agent talked about a substantial salary increase, and guaranteed promotions thereafter. I had obtained a Master's degree in Business through the Central Michigan University on site campus, so I was well qualified for the job. He wanted a commitment from me to fly out to Hartford, Connecticut within a week. I told no one about the job offer because I did not want to be persuaded either way. I wanted to hear only from the Lord, and I needed confirmation quickly. I was faced with two life-changing opportunities. As I sat at my kitchen table that night deliberating about my decision, the Lord brought this passage to my mind:

"For whoever wants to be my disciple must deny themselves and take up their cross and follow me. For whoever wants to save their life will lose it. But whoever loses their life for me will find it. What good will it be for someone to gain the whole world, yet forfeit their soul? Or what can anyone give in exchange for their soul? (Matthew 16:24-26)

While still sitting at the table I typed a letter to the recruiting agent in Hartford, Connecticut declining the new job offer. I put a stamp on the letter and walked out to the front of my apartment complex and dropped it in the mailbox that night. Even if I became tempted later to change my mind, I could not retrieve the letter declining the new job.

Next to my decision to accept Christ as my Savior and Lord in March 1973; declining that new job offer in 1977 to go into full-time ministry was the next most important decision in my life. I am convinced that most of my life blessings, and many of my family's generational blessings, that we enjoy today are based upon this pivotal life-changing decision that I made 38 years ago. Yes, my family and I suffered financial need and lack sometimes during the years that followed; and yes, there were times when I wondered if God was going to provide. But I still have no regrets today, and I would make that same decision again.

Lessons Learned

1. *I believe that the primary determinant of the quality of life we live, is the choices and decisions we make. I also believe that at some point during the course of everyone's life they are confronted by the Spirit of God, and called upon to make a decision to follow or not follow God.*

2. *The blessings that come from serving God and people cannot be counted, nor measured in worldly terms. But they can be counted in the quality of one's life. Serving God and people has made my life richer.*

Of course, I must confess that having lost my wife, Faye the year before, made the decision of resigning my job and enrolling in seminary much easier. After that loss, the meaning of life changed drastically for me. Especially the meaning of money and success, which I believe are the primary stumbling blocks for Christians in America. I used the money that I had saved for a business venture to enroll in Bible college.

In the final analysis, when seemingly unfair and unexplainable things happen in our lives, we have to dig deep, and pray for enough faith to keep believing in God's love, and the goodness of His plan and purpose even while we hurt. We must declare as Job did in the midst of his suffering: "the Lord gives, and the Lord takes, blessed be the name of the Lord..." though He kill me, yet will I trust Him...."after I have been tested, I will come forth as gold (Job 1:21; 13:15; 23:10). Faith that is never tested will be weak, just like an athlete who does not exercise.

Now trust me, making this kind of declaration in the midst of suffering and loss is the most difficult faith action you will ever attempt to do. But, if you can dig deep, and find enough faith and strength to "push through the pain," you will experience a new elevated walk with God that you may not have believed was possible before. You will never see life the same again! Many trivial things won't matter anymore; you will cease to focus on pettiness, your purpose and meaning in life will escalate to a higher level. You will become a person God can use to help carry out His master plan. C.S. Lewis, a great Christian writer, recorded his deep emotional pain and torment, after the death of his wife in his book, *"A Grief Observed", 1961.* I believe that God severely test every true man or woman of God before or during his ministry life. A similar quote by an unknown author reads: "In order for God to use men mightily, He first has to wound them severely."

Preparation for Ministry

In January 1978, I moved from Detroit to Grand Rapids to enroll in seminary. The afternoon that I left Detroit to make the two hour drive to Grand Rapids seemed like another test of faith. There was a snow blizzard. I could hardly see the interstate, and I could only drive about 30 miles per hour. So a two hour trip turned into a four hour trip. But I had to do it! It was imperative that I enroll in school on Monday. Not only that, there were too many potential distractions for me as a new, young, 25 year old widower. I was unaccustomed to that life-style, I needed to leave Detroit for my own sanctification and restoration.

Connecting with a New Home Church

When I arrived in Grand Rapids in 1978, there was only one recommended African-American evangelical church and pastor in town, Starlon Washington at Community Bible Baptist Church. It so happened that the second story apartment that I moved into on Fulton Street was only one block away from the church. So, I could walk there, and I had no reason to go looking elsewhere it was a good place to be. I was welcomed and accepted by the small congregation of about 75 people. Pastor Washington was a good Bible teacher, but his natural gift was evangelism. The church had a strong community outreach ministry.

The city of Grand Rapids happened to be an evangelical stronghold. It was the home of three major Christian publishing companies in the U.S. (Baker, Zondervan, Eerdmans), there were three Bible colleges (Grand Rapids School of the Bible and Music, Calvin College, and Grand Rapids Baptist College and two seminaries (Calvin Seminary and Grand Rapids Baptist Seminary), in addition, Grand Rapids was a strong Dutch Reformed community. For these reasons, the city attracted many men who were preparing for ministry as adult students. There were five of us at Community Church (Charlie Selmon, James Smith, Norm Peart, Luke Wilson, Clagett Ward; some of us became lifelong friends) For these reasons, Grand Rapids proved to be an ideal place to study and prepare for ministry. The theological resources for studying were enormous, and I had lots of male fellowship. But, I was lonely without a wife.

While at Community Church, I began to serve and develop my ministry skills. First, I taught a teen boys Sunday School class, while mentoring another young man, Donald Walker who later became an elder of the church. Secondly, I saw a need in the church to teach young adult Christians dating, pre-marital, and marriage principles. So, I was given permission to start a young adults Sunday School class to focus on these issues. This became a popular class, and several church couples who were dating made decisions to get married. Thirdly, as an Associate Minister, I worked with the pastoral leadership team to develop a strategic plan for the future growth and development of the church. My business planning skill set proved to be one of my most valuable spirit gifts for new church development.

Theological Studies a New Challenge

I had always been a good student, and I loved learning, but I found the study of theology to be a new and different kind of challenge, even though I had already obtained a master degree in Business Management. Nothing in my liberal arts or business education had prepared me for seminary. The terminology was totally foreign to me; I had never heard of words like: *hermeneutics, eschatology, predestination, apologetics, ecclesiology, Calvinism, Arminianism, cosmological argument, fundamentalism, immutability, inerrancy, etc.* I carried a Baker's Dictionary of Theology to every class for the first year, just so I could understand seminary terminology.

I later learned that most of the younger white students in my classes had already graduated from Bible college, and they were there for graduate studies. Which means they had already studied the basics that I was struggling to learn. In addition, I had been out in the work world for seven years before enrolling in seminary. Many of these kids had never held a real

job, except maybe youth ministers on their church staff. Nevertheless, I was accustomed to life challenges, and I knew how to persevere. So, I buried my head in
the books, spent three and half years in every library and bookstore in Grand Rapids, spent every day in class, and every night in the basement studying, and every weekend writing term papers.

Added to this intellectual trauma was the fact that a master degree from most universities in any subject required the completion of only 30 semester hours, but the Master of Divinity degree required the completion of 96 semester hours. And why do I need to know Greek and Hebrew to pastor a church anyway? It seemed like pure torture to me, and I often wondered if those seminary professors were saved, the way they packed assignments into the syllabuses; it seemed like they missed the spiritual gift of compassion. We students jokingly called the school the "cemetery", where they killed aspiring ministers and pastors for three years, and resurrected them for graduation.

Nevertheless, I finished a three year program in three and a half years, going full-time, and graduated with a solid "B" average. In spite of the hardship, it was the best education I ever received, and it was worth the torture. But with all due respect, the Campus Crusade evangelism and discipleship training which I received back in Detroit at the Mission, and the community outreach work we did proved to be equally as helpful in my church planting ministries years later as my seminary education. I was blessed to have both types of training.

From Selma to Salvation

White Evangelicals Financially Supported Black Mission Work

But in the north, by the 1970s coalitions were developing between white evangelicals, and emerging black evangelicals across the U.S. centered on new church planting. This coalition probably was in some ways connected to the issue of segregation in American churches that surfaced during the Civil Rights Movement in the south a decade earlier.

This partnership allowed young black evangelicals to obtain Bible college education and financial support to become full-time ministers. White evangelicals began to see black communities in America as mission fields, and they supported that vision financially for over three decades, in the 1970s thru the 1990s. Most black evangelicals including myself, who served in full-time ministry during this period of time were supported by white evangelical individuals and churches. Very few African-American Christians and churches financially supported black evangelical church planting in those days. In my opinion there was clearly a cultural divide in America, between black and white churches and their understanding of the "Great Commission - go therefore into all the world and make disciples" (Matthew 28:18-20). For black churches, the evangelistic emphasis appeared to be "annual revivals" focused on their own congregation and communities. White evangelicals on the other hand promoted a further evangelistic outreach to the black communities and to foreign mission fields.

On the other hand, this difference in evangelistic perspectives could have been due to several other reasons: 1. historical segregation in America probably forced black churches to stay within the boundaries of their own communities. 2. White Christians literally had more financial resources to spend on evangelistic outreach than blacks. However, the trend of white evangelicals financially supporting black urban church planting efforts begin to decline in the 2000 era. Also, by this time a substantial number of black evangelical churches had become self-supporting, and many black pastors no longer needed white support.

Chapter Nine

A New Helper & A New Ministry Assignment

The Lord Gives Me Another Helper

All study and no play made Junnus a dull boy in Grand Rapids in 1978. I was still relatively new in town, one evening the guys from Community Church invited me to the gym to play basketball. A youth outreach ministry, Christian Development Center (CDC) directed by Clagett Ward was conducting a sports program for church and community kids. While I was playing ball with the guys, I noticed an attractive young lady coaching the girls in volleyball at the opposite end of the gym. I asked one of the guys who she was, and they told me her name was Bonnie.

A few Sundays later, I saw her again at church. Close up she looked even better. So, for a minute, I stepped out of my minister's role, back into my HBCU (historical black college & universities) college boy role to develop a plan to meet Bonnie. Well, no I didn't sin, but I must admit the plan was a bit slick. On this Sunday, I sat in the back of the church to make sure I was behind her, which means when church dismissed, she had to pass by me to get out of the building. Sure enough, she walked by, and I greeted her and introduced myself. She was pleasant, smiled and returned the greeting.

Plan # 1 succeeded, I had met her, she knew my name, and I knew hers. Now for Plan #2. I wanted her phone number, but I had just met her, and it would have been rude to ask her for a phone number so quickly, after all I was no longer a college boy, I was now in seminary studying to be a minister, so I did not want to come off too bold. But neither did I want to wait for another chance encounter to see Bonnie again. So I developed Plan #2. I had been at the church long enough to know the church secretary, Theresa Tillman. She was also one of the single ladies in the church. So, I called the church office one day, and asked her if it would be out of order to ask for Bonnie's phone number; she laughed said "no she didn't think that would be out of order, and she gave me the number from the church directory. Since I had not completed new members' class yet, I did not have a church directory.

Well, the rest is history. Bonnie and I dated for six months. Later during the summer of 1978 she flew down to Selma, Alabama where I was living and conducting family Bible studies to meet my family. Back in Grand Rapids, I had met some members of her family, but not her parents. In July, I was planning to drive to Dallas, Texas for a Christian Conference, and I asked her to attend. She agreed, but we had to work out one small travel detail. How were we going to travel and stay together for an entire week, as an unmarried couple, and avoid a moral failure? Once we weighed all of our options, there was only one solution. Get married! So, we planned a destination wedding in Dallas. When we got to Dallas, we called Bonnie's parents back in Baldwin, Michigan. I specifically spoke to her father, T.L. Anderson, and asked permission to marry his daughter.

He jokingly said, "She is grown, and free to make her own decisions" (we were 27 years old). Then he gave us his blessings. The conference was being held on Bishop College campus. Several of my minister friends who were associated with Campus Crusade were there, and so were a group of my church family members from the Mission in Detroit. We had enough people to make up a good wedding party. On July 6, 1978 we were married in the Bishop College Chapel. My family gave us a small reception once we returned to Selma; Bonnie's family and our church family also gave us a large dinner reception when we returned back to Grand Rapids in August.

One year later, our first child, Davida was born; three years later on the exact day of our third wedding anniversary, July 6th, our second daughter, Claressa was born. Bonnie was a great mother and homemaker. She took good care of our children, and our family. For me having another wife, children and a family of my own was another form of healing and restoration from the Lord, after losing Faye in 1976. I could now see the light of God in my life again, and it felt great

---

Lessons Learned

1. *We must trust God and follow Him even when we don't understand the "life changes" we may be going through.*

2. *Remember that God always has a higher purpose, and a higher plan for your life than you can see. The only way you will ever know His plan for your life, and experience the joy and blessing of walking in it is to "trust and obey!"*

3. *Isaiah 55: 8,9 has been one of the foundational Scriptures of my spiritual journey with God:*

"For my thoughts are not your thoughts, neither are your ways my ways" declares the Lord. "As the heavens are higher than the earth, so are my ways higher than your ways and my thoughts higher than your thoughts."

As I look back over our 30 years of marriage and ministry together, Bonnie proved to be the ideal wife, mother and ministry partner. As the oldest daughter, and sometimes mother figure of her family (the Andersons), she was seasoned and mature beyond her years; as a charter member of Community Church in Grand Rapids, she also had new church planting experience which was my ministry focus.

From Selma to Salvation

Relocating Back to Alabama for Ministry

By the time I graduated from seminary in May 1981, my heart was firmly set on planting a new church in Selma. And I was fairly certain that this was my new assignment from the Lord. So, I started networking to make the right connection for getting back to Alabama. I needed a group of supporting churches, or a denomination to financially support the project and to endorse the move back to Alabama. This would be a sure sign to me that God was really leading in this move. After all, I was married now, and had a family to support. So I had to balance my call and zeal for ministry with my responsibility to financially support the family. I was passionate about relocating to Alabama, but I would not move without confirmation from the Lord.

Finally, in the fall of 1982, God revealed my first ministry assignment: Ensley Bible Church, in Birmingham; to my disappointment, it was not Selma. But Birmingham was close enough. It was only 90 miles from Selma, so I could still reach out to my people in Selma, and they could drive up to participate in some Sunday services. Ensley Bible Church was an aborted church plant attempted by a group of black evangelical ministers from of Dallas, Texas: Dr. Reuben Conner, Willie Peterson, Tony Evans, and Eddie Lane. They operated under the name Black Evangelistic Enterprise (BEE), the name was later changed to Urban Evangelical Mission (UEM) sometimes in the 1990s. They had planted several successful Bible churches in the Dallas area that served as good models, and training stationed for the young pastors they were recruiting, and the future churches they hoped to start.

When, Bonnie, myself, and our two children Davida and Claressa arrived at Ensley Bible Church there were about 40 members, who were meeting in a storefront building on Avenue F in the Ensley area. Financially, they could only afford to pay me a part-time salary, but Bonnie was a school teacher, so we were able to meet our expenses. Demographically, the church was not a progressive group, they had grown content, and operated in a maintenance mode; their reputation within the city as an aborted church plant was not good. I, on the other hand was a progressive minded, goal-oriented new young pastor, fresh out of seminary with lots of new ideas. My progressive style was at times overwhelming for them, but eventually they made the adjustment, began to follow my leadership, and became great supporters of my vision as the pastor.

Word spread around Birmingham about the new young fiery preacher at Ensley Bible Church, and new people began to visit the church. Some old members who had left in disappointment at the first pastor's moral fall, returned.
My immediate goal was to relocate the church to a decent facility, and a better neighborhood as soon as possible. The largest and closest housing community was the Ensley Projects. As the pastor, I was somewhat embarrassed by both the facility and the location, I feared that this location would hinder the church's growth. We would not be able to attract competent members to help us build a self-supporting church. Nevertheless some progressive people from across the city began to attend the church.

I worked hard at Ensley Bible Church teaching, caring and getting to know the people. My wife, Bonnie had the gift of hospitality, and she loved inviting church members to the house on Sunday afternoons, which also provided new friends for our children Davida and Claressa. In the meantime, our third child, Simeon, decided to arrive. I had hoped for a son before now. The fact that our third child was a boy made his surprised arrival easier to embrace.

Being a home boy from Alabama, and having attended a black college, Alabama A&M proved to be a plus, especially with the men in the church. The annual magic city football classic, between Alabama State and Alabama A&M was the largest gathering of black people in the South, and it was held at Legion Field in Birmingham. So, as a marketing strategy, I used football game talk to motivate the men in the church. We also had an early morning racquetball team of church men that played at the UAB gym. I was a competitive athlete, so again, I used sports to motivate my church men to become more involved. And they did.

Lessons Learned

1. One of the Keys to a Pastor's Success is surrounding himself with Good Men; and I Do Mean "Men", not Women.

2. After learning how to conduct men discipleship groups, I formed men house-to-house study groups in each one of my ministry locations. Men must be recruited to Christ one-by-one. They rarely walk down the aisle in response to a sermon.

I formed a bond with the men of Ensley Bible Church that went for beyond me being their pastor. To this day, we are brothers in Christ and our families are friends: James Nation, Gerard Boone, David Jones, Jr (deceased), Ken Reese, and Lawrence Robinson are men of God who I commend for their service to God, and admire for their life-time Christian commitment. They served as leaders with me for six years, and they have supported me in difficult times since then, as their brother in Christ. Paul's exhorted Timothy to hold men like these in "high esteem", and I do! These men, self-admittedly, are far from perfect, but they are examples of what "true elders and deacons" in a church should be. I would not attempt to pastor a church today without men like these standing beside me.

A New Church, A New Location

One of my God-given, natural gifts is the ability to plan, launch, and develop new organizations. In the business world this is called "organizational development." This gift also includes the ability to properly assess the state and status of existing organizations, and developing "strategic plans" for their future success. Unfortunately, most African-American churches, as well as many others, do not apply these business principles to their churches even when they are available. As a result, most churches in America today are declining, losing members, and dying. Which I believe is a waste of Kingdom assets and resources.

Within two years, I had built a strong enough bond with the elders, and the people to start promoting a relocation. We found an older Presbyterian church building in West End that was ideal. We started a fund-raising campaign, but our small group, which had grown to about 50 members now was only able to raise about $5,000 as a down payment on the building after three months. It wasn't much but I was still willing to move forward and trust God.

So, I put the business negotiation skills that I had learned in government contracting to work for God. The elders and myself called a meeting with the white Presbyterian leaders of the West End church, and presented them a written offer to lease-purchase the building for $5,000 and $500 per month, for

3 years. We were not in a financial position to offer a realistic purchase price, which probably would have been in the $250,000 range. So, we only offered a lease-purchase with a commitment to negotiate a full purchase after 3 years. There congregation size had dwindled down to less than 10 older adults; they had no children in the church, the new baby nursery in the education building they had built a few years earlier had never been used. They really wanted to get rid of the building, and I also believed that God had put it on their hearts to help this small young black church succeed. They accepted our offer.

Everyone was excited! Especially me, the Pastor. Our little storefront church was on the move. God had blessed the vision and plan I had laid out. The members of Ensley Bible Church felt vindicated. They were now finally able to move pass the old stigma of being a failed church that was just marking time, but going nowhere. Thirty days after signing a contract with West End Presbyterian, we planned a move-in. Our move-in to the new church was preceded by an advertisement campaign through-out the city of Birmingham. We planned a "friends and family" day, with food being served in our new spacious fellowship hall which could easily seat over 100 people. We planned a motor car caravan from the old church cite to the new church site. The Birmingham Times newspaper came out to report on our first service.

An important part of our new move was a church name change: we dropped the old "Ensley Bible Church" name with all its stigmas, and chose the new name: "New Covenant Bible Baptist Church." We added "Baptist" to our name to identify with the Afro-American audience we were seeking to reach. Black people in Birmingham in 1980 had never heard of a "Bible" church. During community evangelism, we spent more time explaining what a Bible church was, than we did talking about the Gospel.

As a New Young Pastor I Needed a Mentor

I felt I was making good progress in the Birmingham church, even though it was my first pastorate. Yet, because I had been trained in discipleship as a new Christian back in Detroit, I saw the need for pastoral discipleship as a new pastor. I needed a senior pastor to consult with concerning the many variables, factors and decisions of pastoring a church. So, I called our largest supporting white church in Birmingham, Briarwood Presbyterian (PCA). Pastor Frank Barker had been a friend of our church since its beginning. In addition, he was a kind, gentle, humble man who was committed to disciplining men, even though he was responsible for a church of over 5,000 members. My church only had about 100 members at the time, But Frank never made me feel like my small church problems were unimportant. I asked Frank if he had ever done pastoral discipleship. He said no, but he would be willing to try.

So, we starting meeting once each month in my church office. Frank never came with a prepared script or lesson to teach or talk to me about. He came to listen. He simply asked, Junnus, what do you want to talk about today? I would have a list of the personal and church issues that were concerning me, and he would talk through the pros and cons of every issue. He never told me "what to do," he would only say: "try this," try that," "think about that," or "see how that works." It was very wise counsel, he always left room for the spirit of God to teach and lead me.

Frank also bought me lunch at a nearby restaurant each time met, once each month. These meetings continued for a about one year. It is because of the kindness that Frank Barker, a white Presbyterian minister showed me, that I make an effort to assist and encourage young pastors as often as possible. Accepting the call to be a minister/pastor is one of the most difficult jobs any man or women will ever attempt to do.

In 1985, and for several years after changing our name, and moving into our new facility, the Birmingham church was progressive and moved forward. Our membership grew from 50 to 150; we opened a day care center, started a Christian school and began to offer services to our new West End community. As an educator, my wife Bonnie, gave up her job and became the full-time director of our church education program. We hired other educators who were members our church: Sharon Williams, Octavia Davis and Lavert Agee (deceased). We began educating our own children, as well as other children from the community in both Christian and academic education. Charles and Jerrie Lewis had also joined our staff by this time as Evangelism Directors. The church continued to grow, and attracted new families with education, skills, and resources for serving God and people. One of those stand-out couples were Wendal (deceased 2014) and Marguerite Scott; they supported my ministries for years, even after leaving the Birmingham church.

Lessons Learned

God is the Author of Unity, But Satan Makes Continuous Attempts to Bring Division within the Church (Matthew 16: 17-19)

Jesus exhorted His disciples to "watch and pray" so that they would not fall into temptation (Matthew 26:41). After five years of hard work at the Birmingham church, and reaching a pinnacle of success: a day care center, a Christian school, a growing, thriving congregation of 150-200 members, and several full-time paid staff workers, our church suffered a split, and we lost half of our members. This split came through debates about the "Charismatic Movement", a new sensationalism based church movement that swept across the U.S. in the 1980's, especially taking root in African-American communities where church folks had not been taught sound Bible doctrine. New Charismatic churches were springing up in Birmingham, with the new teachings of: "prosperity", "speaking in tongues" and "healing." This was a highly emotionally charged teaching, sometimes comically referred to as the "name it and claim it" movement. Our church taught the conservative Bible doctrine of "salvation, by faith, through grace. (Ephesians 2:8, 9). We believed the Bible taught that "miraculous signs" were limited primarily to the Apostolic age (Peter, James, John, Paul in the Bible), and were used as authenticating signs of the Gospel of Jesus Christ for "unbelievers" in the early church (1 Corinthians 14; 22).

These gifts were not for "believers." Nor were they to have a major role in the church today like teaching, preaching, evangelism and prayer would have. In other words, our church taught that being able to "speaking in tongues" was not proof of salvation, nor evidence of having a deeper connection with God. We taught that "healing" power did not reside with any individuals, but only with God, who healed according to His Will, and that God's primary purpose for Christians was not for us to seek "money", but to be dedicated to loving and serving one another (1 Timothy 6:9), and winning unsaved people to Christ (Matthew 28: 18-20).

On the positive side, the new charismatic churches brought exciting "praise and worship" programs to the churches, which I believe were much needed, and very attractive to youth and young adults who were turned-off by old church hymns like "Amazing Grace." So, on the one hand, the new churches were doing good, by reaching the younger generation who had stopped attending traditional churches, as I did at age 17. On the other hand, they were teaching "false doctrine." People were coming to charismatic churches so that God would "bless them" with money, healing, success, etc. Rather than coming to church seeking God in humble repentance of their sins, and learning how to live a Spirit-filled life that demonstrated the fruit of the Spirit: love, joy, peace, patience, goodness, gentleness, faith, and self-control.

Many of the newer members who joined New Covenant Church around 1985 were charismatic sympathizers, who embraced our conservative doctrine during the new members' orientation classes, but later turned, and tried to spread the charismatic doctrine through-out our church. These people arrogantly thought that they had better insight, wisdom, and an anointing from God and the Holy Spirit that neither I, the pastor, nor the elders, nor any of our long time church members had. In other words, God had sent them to our church "to deliver us from ignorance, and bring us into the light!" Frankly speaking, this level of arrogance was fueled by ignorance, and I believe incited by Satan himself against the church. And it angered me! "I wanted to literally throw them all out!" But the elders, and I waited and prayed for God to restore harmony within the church. Unfortunately, that didn't happened.

I, as pastor, and the elders stood against this disruption within the church. Two of our new elder wives became out spoken charismatic sympathizers within the church. Our leadership team met with these elders and their wives, in an attempt to bring them back into harmony, and restore unity within our church, but they would not be persuaded. We voted to remove these men as elders. This move caused a ripple effect reaction within the church among people who liked these two elders. Nevertheless, these disruptive and rebellious people needed to be removed from our church.

Lessons Learned

Division in the Church and Losing Members Breaks a Pastor's Heart

A true pastor loves the people in his church, just as much as he loves his own family members; sometimes even more. If those people have been members for years, then the pastor has been intricately involved in their lives: their weddings, the birth of their children, the graduations of their children, counseling them through marriage problems, divorces, sickness, unemployment, the death of loved ones, and sometimes, even the death of favorite members. The breaking of these types of relationships weigh heavy on a pastor's heart. Such was the case for me, at the Birmingham church. My heart was broken by the church division and the loss of members. Nevertheless, in these days and time, all churches will lose members; membership rotation is a common phenomenon in our contemporary culture. Unfortunately, some church people are only loyal to the newest, and most exciting pastor or church in town.

For six years, Bonnie and I had worked hard to reach, teach and care for our people, we loved them all, and their families, including the disruptive ones. But in order to save the church, we had to let some members go, and in order to save ourselves, we had to leave after losing so much, we could not bear to stay and watch our church decline any further.

Lessons Learned

1. Hold good pastors and ministers in high esteem.

2. To church people, if you happen to be in a good church with a good pastor; encourage and support the pastor and his family. They shoulder a heavy burden that none of the members will ever understand. Pastoring and serving God's people is a labor of love; it is a unique calling; just as Christ suffered, every truly called man and woman of God will also suffer, providing sacrificial serve to the people of God. Hold these people in high esteem (Philippians 2:29)

3. Be Alert, there is a Judas in every church

Judas was one of Christ's disciples, but he was also a betrayer. In every church, there is probably a Judas, hiding among God's people and pretending to be a true believer. When in reality he is an agent of Satan waiting for an opportunity to do the Devil's work of destroying people and relationships in the church. Church leaders need to be alert, aware and protect the people from the betrayers in the church.

There will always be a group of sympathizers in the church who wants to "keep everyone together in the name of love and unity." But understand that "unity" in the body will only be short lived until the Judas in the church is discovered and removed. A word of caution: people should only be expelled from the church when

> *there is "no other solution." The Pastor and elders must act prayerfully, carefully and wisely in this matter (Titus 2:15-3:10; Acts 20:28-31).*

A decade after the "Charismatic Movement" swept our cities, communities, and churches, we began to see some of the fall out. Many of these young charismatic preachers came on the scene with little or no theological education, or pastoral training, they built megachurches based upon their flamboyant personalities, with TV ministries, driving luxury cars, wearing tailored suits, living in upscale homes in the suburbs, with trophy wives, proclaiming themselves the CEOs (chief executive officers)of Christ's church, and appointing their wives and family members CFOs (chief financial officer); using God's church as their own private business enterprises, taking advantage of God's people, and "acting like celebrities in Hollywood, rather than God's humble servants in the hood."

After a while, God Himself began to speak, as He always does to set the record straight, defend His name, and protect His Church. During the past two decades we have seen certain pastors and ministers constantly in the news for various kinds of moral failures: divorces, sexual immorality, financial mismanagement, IRS investigations, domestic violence, and in a few cases death by hand guns in the church, and possible drug overdose.

Because I travel in pastors circles, I happen to know of others minister failures that have never made the news. Thank God! None of us in the body of Christ like to see these kinds of moral failures happen; because none of us are exempt. It can happen to anyone. All of us, pastors and ministers must learn to be careful and accountable (Galatians 6:1-10).

Lessons Learned

1. *Every Pastor Needs A Pastor – for accountability and counsel.*

2. *The primary reason the Bible needs to be taught within the church is so that untrained, untaught new believers are not so easily persuaded by false teaching.*

3. *I strongly advise all new and young pastors, not to attempt to do ministry as an independent man, unaccountable to a senior minister, a supporting church association or a denomination. None of us are wise or spiritual enough to stand against the offense of Satan alone. He will work to defeat you every day, unless you are accountable and submissive to some other godly men, you will fall, it's just a matter of time (I Peter 5:6-9).*

4. *A great book on this subject is: "Overcoming the Dark Side of Leadership," Gary McIntosh, Baker Books, 2007*

In 1988, after being burned-out, stressed-out, and suffering major setbacks at the Birmingham church I resigned to rest and refocus. I worked with the elders and BEE in Dallas, Texas to help recruit a new pastor for the church. I remained until the next pastor was installed. At this point I was not sure, if God was using the Birmingham church's decline to force me to Selma, or if Satan was the architect, and defeated us through doctrinal division. Either way, I had time on my hand, and no Sunday ministry, so I started commuting to Selma two Sundays each month. After all, Selma was my original destination when I returned to Alabama. Even then, God was confirming my calling to be a Church Planter, that would move regularly, rather than a Pastor that would remain with one congregation long-term. Still, it was only after serving in ministry for two decades that I truly accepted my unique calling.

Chapter Ten

Returning Home to Serve My People

From Selma to Salvation

Family Bible Studies in Selma -Laying a Church Foundation

During the period 1975 to 1978, I have already referred to the fact that I took regular opportunities during my visits to Selma to share as much Christian literature and Bible information with my family members as possible. During the summer of 1978, my first summer break during seminary, I actually lived in Selma for the entire summer teaching Bible studies. The driving force behind this plan and approach was that I recognized the level of Bible knowledge, and Christian training among the black population in Selma was woefully lacking. I observed that many people were in church as I had been growing up there, but they were not receiving any Christian training about "how to actually be saved, and live the Christian life."

With all due respect, this is not a criticism of the black churches is Selma, but an observation. I found that the same situation existed in many black churches outside of the Selma, in other cities and states. "Black people were very religious, and very faithful to their churches," but back in the 70's many black pastors were not theologically educated or trained in "evangelism, discipleship, or biblical expository preaching." However, this situation is greatly improved today, in 2015. So, in actuality, a person could be a church member all of their lives, be a good God-fearing person, but never "have the assurance of salvation," simply because of cultural traditions, and lack of training. Which is exactly what happening to me as a youth growing up in church. With better Christian education, I probably would have made better decisions, and may not have taken the five year hiatus from church that I did.

The problem within the black church in Selma was not willful disobedience, but a lack of knowledge. I found the people and the pastors to be humble seekers of God's will and God's way. Once, I understood what I had missed growing up in Mt. Ararat Baptist Church in east Selma; I now believed that a part of my call to ministry by God was to bring more enlightenment to this situation. This enlightenment was to come by starting and establishing a new church that more adequately addressed people's personal and spiritual needs. Including, learning and studying the Bible, having access to pastoral counseling for personal problems, and being taught how to live the Christian life-style as a saved person, rather than just being a church member. Under no circumstances would I criticize, or attempt to change the old ways of church and religion in Selma. My goal was simply to start "a new way of teaching, preaching and conducting church," and those who were impressed by the Spirit of God would be drawn to the new way.

There would never be any attempt to "steal sheep", or lead people who were comfortable in their traditional churches away. The type of new Bible teaching church I would offer was designed to be an alternative only for those who were seeking and open to a new and different way to make a God connection. This new church planting movement among blacks was already happening in the north, in fact Bonnie and I met in this type of church. But it had not yet made it to small towns in the South, like Selma.

A House Church - commuting from Birmingham to Selma

In 1988, after resigning from New Covenant in Birmingham, our family started making the 90 mile drive to Selma two Sundays each month. The initial Bible studies were held at Jerald and Anita's (my brother-in-law/sister)house since they had the largest living areas. The first meetings included only family members, but we still averaged 15 to 20 people. We purposefully did not invite outsiders because our space was limited. Commuting to Selma to be with family two times a month proved to be good for me, Bonnie and the children after the intense six years of work we had done at the Birmingham church. We needed emotional, mental and physical restoration.

We met house to house in Selma for a few years, then we rented the Kiddie Kastle Day Care Building from Ms. Gifford on Highland Avenue. At this point, we started to have more organized church services with praise and worship in addition to the Bible teaching. The Selma Church stayed at the Kiddie College location for about two years. More people began to attend, growth and development was slow but steady.
The Sunday only ministry with family was good, but during the week back in Birmingham I had family obligations.

I thought the Lord may be leading me from Alabama to another assignment; so, I applied for ministry jobs outside of Alabama to test God's direction. I received two offers: 1. Black Ministries Director, for William Tyndale Bible College in Detroit, Michigan 2. Associate Director of Church Planting, Black Evangelistic Enterprise (BEE), in Dallas, Texas. Since, I had been a full-time Pastor in Birmingham, I needed to find another source of income for the family. Our Christian school had already closed, so Bonnie was teaching public school at this time, and all three of the children were attending W.J. Christian School, where she taught, so my resignation did not drastically upset the family.

A New Ministry Job – Still in Birmingham

Both of the new ministry job offers were problematic: 1. moving to either Detroit or Dallas would have required uprooting the family, and after doing some research, I discovered that neither job offered much long-term financial security. But before, declining the Detroit offer, I asked Bonnie if she wanted to relocate closer to her home and family back in Michigan. She liked the warm weather in the south, and did not want to return to Michigan. So, I declined both job offers.
After a few months had passed, I received a phone call from Pastor Sam Pettagrue at Sardis Baptist Church in Birmingham. As two pastors in the city of Birmingham, Sam and I had a cordial relationship based upon our mutual connection with Pastor Frank Barker of Briarwood Presbyterian Church.

Once Sam found out I had resigned from my church, and knowing about my organizational development and grant writing experience, he asked me to come over to Sardis, and help him develop a Christian Resource Center. The church was also launching a Christian school. Sardis Baptist was a large middle class black church, and they had sufficient resources to pay my salary, while I helped raise grant funds. Historically, Sardis was a traditional church, but Sam had broken out of traditionalism, and was becoming a more progressive, innovative pastor. He was exposing his people to new Christian teaching and training. He was also a gentle, kind man, I liked being around him, so I agreed to work with him. But I made no commitment to Sardis Church ministry. I was only hired to work on the CRC project. This was a win-win for me, because I could still commute to the Selma church two Sundays each month.

Selma Community Bible Church – is officially incorporated

In 1991, the home Bible studies and family worship services that I had been conducting itinerantly was officially organized into a church. During the past thirteen years, I had spent in-depth time teaching and training two faithful men. Lecester Strong and Jerald Stallworth. Incidentally, they both happened to be my brothers-in-law, married to two of my sisters. So, they were compelled to support my vision (just joking). Over the years, these men had been exposed to some substantial training and discipleship. They had traveled regularly to the Birmingham church to see a model of an evangelical Bible church in operation. I felt they were ready to lead.

On occasions, I had taken some of the elders and associate pastors from Birmingham down to Selma to help conduct leadership training. The Selma pastors' interpretation and teaching of the Scriptures were accurate. So, I convened an ordination council of elders and pastors, examined these men, and licensed and ordained them. After the ordination of Pastors Strong and Stallworth, to oversee the Selma church, I reduced my commuting to Selma to once each month. They needed the experience of overseeing and conducting the work of the church without my presence.

The Selma church leased a small church building on Martin L. King drive in 1995 and met there for about 10 years. During this ten year period of time, the church maintained and grew slowly. Several major events occurred that shook the very foundation of the church, as well as our faith as a family, but God was faithful, and kept the church standing through it all:

- In 1991 I accepted a new church planting assignment in Houston, Texas; my family and I left Birmingham. I felt the church had a strong foundation, and two capable pastors. They were in good hands.

- In 1996, my mother, Leola Clay, the mother of the Selma church who had left her traditional home church at Mt. Ararat Baptist died.

- In 2000, Pastor Lecester Strong, the first official pastor of the Selma church passed away suddenly. The church was obviously devastated, by his sudden passing. I, having already relocated back to Atlanta at this time, begin to commute back to Selma two times per month, to serve as interim pastor until Jerald Stallworth was installed as the new pastor in 2001.

- In 2002, we lost Anita Clay Stallworth, my sister, the wife of Pastor Stallworth, and the first lady of the church to breast cancer after a brief two year battle.

Upon This Rock, I Will Build My Church

In spite of several years of severe hardship and loss, Pastor Stallworth, and the members of Selma Community Bible Church continued in their faith. Sometime around 1997, they bought a plot of land on Highway 14 East; in 2003 they broke ground for their own church building, and in 2004 they held their first worship service in the new building. This accomplishment was a tremendous achievement considering the numerous setbacks they suffered. But the resilience of this small church is a testament to their sincere faith in God, and His almighty power to heal.

From Selma to Salvation

The last time I preached at my home church in October 2014, I looked out over the congregation and noted that there were three generations of my own family members sitting in the audience being taught the Word of God. Whenever, any of my older aunts visit we reach back to four generations.

This book "From Selma to Salvation" is a God story. He is the author and I am the actor, reading and following the script that He wrote for my life. It is a story about how the sovereignty of God allowed me to stand on the Edmund Pettus Bridge in Selma at age 14 and march in the Civil Rights Movement. It tells how that same God transported me to another world to experience salvation, and then He lured me back home to Selma to share the good news of the Gospel to four generations of my relatives through the church that we built. I hope this story inspires you to read and follow the script God has written for your life. Wouldn't you like to know what you were born to do? It promises to be an exciting journey!

Lessons Learned

"Oh, how great are God's riches and wisdom and knowledge! How impossible it is for us to understand His decisions and his ways!" (Romans 11:33 – NLT)

Chapter Eleven

MY HOPE AND PRAYER FOR SELMA

From Selma to Salvation

My Hope and Prayer for Selma is that the City Fathers and Leaders will Figure out How to Leverage the History and Reputation of Selma into more Economic Development and Opportunities for the People and for the City

1. Wherever I go in America today, and some other countries, if people find out that I am a native of Selma, Alabama, there is immediate recognition, and often a "thank you" if they find out I participated in the Civil Rights marches.

2. When I come home to Selma, I would love to see more signs of economic progress and prosperity. I know from history that many jobs and substantial revenue have been loss over the decades as Craig AFB moved out, and the garment factories closed and sent jobs overseas. Many people in Selma are still living below the poverty level. While the annual Jubilee is a great time of remembering our history and celebrating the "fact" that we overcame. And I think it should continue. My question is: "how are the citizens of Selma benefiting from all of the high status celebrities, congressmen, presidents, dignitaries, businessmen, CEOs, etc. who come to town annually for photo opportunities.

3. Forgive my ignorance, and presumption, if this is already being done, but is there some way that the city fathers and leaders can leverage the jubilee event and the reputation of Selma to help provide more long term economic empowerment for the citizens and the city? Entertainers, professional athletes, politicians, and CEOs have access to substantial economic resources. Is this access being used in any way to empower the citizens of Selma? Surely, some of these people are open to help and work together in coalitions and collaborations with the city leaders for more economic empowerment. Surely, the mayor of Selma can appeal to the

President, congressional leaders, and business people who come to town to walk hand in hand with him across the bridge every year.

4. If new auto factories are being located in places like Montgomery, LaGrange, Georgia, Tuscaloosa, etc. surely the city leaders of Selma can get an audience with the board of directors of these companies to solicit more jobs for the people of Selma. If not a major factory, then smaller supply shops can also provide jobs. There are also many job training grants available through the U.S. Dept. of Labor, and private foundations.

5. Progress in a city is usually visible. I travel from Atlanta to Selma at least once every three months. It would bless my heart to see more visible signs of progress in my hometown.
I think it was Dr. King who said, "what good is it, to be able to sit at a lunch counter, if you cannot afford to buy lunch."

6. Finally my prayer and my hope for my hometown and its citizens is that they will experience: "freedom, justice, economic prosperity, spiritual renewal, and the better quality of life that the Civil Rights Movement intended to make possible. This includes: better jobs, housing, social and medical services, education, entertainment, and commercial shopping entities.

From Selma to Salvation

Chapter Twelve

MY HOPE AND PRAYER FOR THE CHURCH

From Selma to Salvation

The Current State of the Local Church

This book is primarily about my spiritual journey, thus the word "Salvation" in the title. A journey that has continued for 37 years. It began in the church, and I hope to complete and end it serving and building the church of Jesus Christ. But before I go any further in this concluding chapter, let me define my usage of the word "Church." In this book, and in the Bible there are basically two definitions of church. 1. the church, small "c" refers to the local churches that we minister in and attend for worship. Most of my references to "church" are referring to local churches. 2. the "Church", capital "C" refers to the universal Church, the entire body of believers; Christians all over the world, being the people of God, and doing Kingdom work in the name of Jesus Christ, our Lord and Savior.

Of the many life and career projects I have done, church work has been the most important, most rewarding, and at the same time most frustrating. A longtime friend, recently asked me a profound question: "if you only had one year to live what would you do?" I have been forced through the circumstances of life to think through that question many times. So, without any hesitation, I said, I would do three things: 1. I would put all of my business affairs in order for my children and family. 2. I would take a traveling tour and say my final good-byes to all of my loves ones and the significant others in my life. 3. I would take every opportunity to tell as many people as I could about the love of Jesus Christ, and encourage them to accept Him as their Savior and Lord.

This is My Calling and Purpose

I thank the Lord that I was blessed by His grace to discover my calling and gifts in life at an early age. I was saved at age 22, and became a minister at age 27. My purpose in life is and has been to serve the Lord, teach His people and build His church. Granted, in my life time, I have done many other projects along the way, but my primary life purpose has never changed. So, this explains why my first book is about my spiritual journey and the church. I was not called by God to be a politician or Civil Rights activist; nor was I sent back to Selma to address those kinds of causes, though they were and are issues that still need to be addressed today. Instead, I was called by God to build local churches.

In addition to the churches I personally served in Japan, Michigan, Alabama, Texas and Georgia; I have been blessed by God during the past 16 years, while living in Georgia to provide start-up consulting serves to over 500 other churches and ministries in the U.S. and several countries (India, Africa, Russia, and the Caribbean Islands) through my consulting company, Resource Development Services (RDS), LLC.

During this same period of time, I also worked part-time on the leadership team of the Southeast District of the Missionary Church USA, Ft. Wayne, Indiana, with Bob Ransom, Dan Palmer, and Hector Soto helping to ordain over 30 new pastors, and starting or restoring over 25 multi-cultural churches (Haitian, Hispanic, Brazilian, African-American, and Caucasian) in the metro Atlanta area.

I don't share this information to boast about my service record in ministry, but to make a statement about how important I believe it is for those of us who are called to serve the church, to "know" and "work" in the places where God assigns us. It took me about two decades to stop second guessing God, and accept the unique aspect of my calling. Because, many times I wanted be a pastor like some of my associates who stayed in one place, and served one church for a life-time.

"Upon this rock, I will build My Church, and the power of Hell will not overcome it (stop it, conquer it, or overpower it) (Matthew 16:18).

It is Important that we understand that the Church of Jesus Christ is a Movement, not an Organization or Institution

The most profound similarity that I have found between the life work of both Jesus Christ and Dr. Martin L. King is that they were both committed primarily to a movement. Not an organization, or institution. A movement is uniquely different in that it is mobile, flexible, its modus operandi (method of operation) is mobilizing people for action in order to accomplish a mission. The end goal of both Christ and Dr. King's movement was a better quality of life for people. In addition, their movements were usually "holistically focused". Both Christ and Dr. King defined their missions similarly as stated in the Scripture below:

"The Spirit of the Lord is upon Me. Because He has anointed Me to preach the gospel to the poor; He has sent Me to heal the brokenhearted, to proclaim liberty to the captives and recovery of sight to the blind, to set at liberty those who are oppressed; to proclaim the acceptable year of the Lord." (Luke 4:18,19)

All of the resources of a movement are directed toward the mission. A movement by nature must travel light, and be ready to mobilize at a moment's notice. It cannot be weighed down by heavy overhead expenses, an unclear mission, multiple agendas, leaders in conflict, etc.

Lessons Learned

I don't think it's ironic that my early life began as part of a "movement." I think it was a part of God's divine plan. I am still called to be part of a "movement." The movement of mobilizing the Church of Jesus Christ to reach, teach, love and serve unreached people in Selma, America, and the World!" As Dr. Benjamin E. Mays, said in his autobiography – "I Wouldn't Take Nothing For My Journey!"

Sadly, in my observations and opinion the church in America is in serious trouble! It is unhealthy, and making less of an impact on the modern day American culture. Especially, youth and young adults. It has lost sight of its mission; it is has ceased to be a movement for Christ, it has become "an overweight, out of shape institution", weighed down by decades and centuries of traditions, history and overhead expenses that are too heavy to carry. An overweight church cannot move quickly when its commander calls; it cannot serve, respond and address the needs of people; it cannot reach out to the poor, oppressed, brokenhearted, and captives because it is encumbered with managing its own internal problems. It has become a self-perpetuating machine that constantly seeks, and need more people to serve its agenda, by giving more money, time and resources to keep the machine operating to accomplish its own mission, not the Great Commission of Christ (Matthew 28; 18-20). Granted, this is a seemingly harsh and critical statement.

Less, I sound too critical of the church and offend some. Let me say, I love the church, and I have dedicated my life to serving it. Also by way of commendations, I have observed that many African-American pastors and churches have drastically improved their theological education, their Christian education programs, and they are consciously "leading people to salvation in Christ," rather than just offering people church membership. Personally, I know some men of God, who are doing great work leading people to Christ, and disciplining them in their churches. So, much has changed in the black church for good since I was saved in 1973, and began working in Selma in 1978. I am in sympathy with the churches in America; they are all being bombarded with difficult moral issues, struggling with social and economic changes that affect their members; and trying to develop strategies to reach new people groups in their communities. I believe most of them really want to a better job in accomplishing their missions.

For a biblical example of what a New Testament movement church should be study Acts 2:41-47. Across America, there are examples and models of ministers and churches that are resisting institutionalization, and are staying "movement" focus. For some examples of these read the writings of Francis Chan, David Platt, Ed Stetzer, Mark Batterson and various articles in "Outreach Magazine."

Specific Issues that need to be addressed

1. the church in America is declining in attendance and membership. Only 20% to 40% of Americans actually attend church today (*churchleaders.com*).

2. Most churches still operate in a traditional program format that caters to the majority of members who are already attending. They do not have a major outreach strategy and programs that are designed to attract non-church goers, unbelievers, or non-Christians, especially the younger generation under age 40.

3. I believe people outside the church see churches as "takers", not "givers", as "looking down" at them, rather than "reaching down" to help lift them up.

4. I believe that in order for the church as institution, to have a substantial impact and influence on the American culture, and reach a substantial number of non-church goers, it will have to drastically change most of its current operations, and major on reaching out to people with practical demonstrations of "love", that address their felt needs.

5. If the church makes the necessary changes, I believe America as a nation will experience a major spiritual revival; if the church does not make the changes, we will continue to see a steady moral decline at all levels of society.

I Believe the Local Church is the Most Important Movement in America, and it is our Only Hope

The Church is the most important movement, and it is the only hope for America. Because it is the only agent in America that possesses the power of God. And only the power of God can save people, America, and the world from the prophetic moral decline, and the apocalyptic doom that the Bible says will come upon the earth in the last days. Study these two important passages: 2 Timothy 3: 1-7; 13; 4:3, 4 ; 2 Peter 3:3-18.

My recommendation to Individuals

My recommendation for you: those I know and love is do not live in panic or fear, continue to live and enjoy the life and blessings God has given you. However, while you live and enjoy life, find the best Bible teaching, movement focused, holistic serving church available, and get involved.

My Recommendations to Pastors and Churches who are interested in Becoming Movement Focused:

1. take a new look at the biblical model of the New Testament Church in Acts 2: 41-47.

2. revisit the Great Commission that Christ commanded his disciples to follow in Matthew 28:18-20; and which He has not yet rescinded, neither has it been fulfilled. And recognized that it is still a mandate for which our Lord will hold us responsible.

3. Re-read the instructions that Jesus gave to his twelve disciples when he sent them out on their first evangelistic mission in Matthew 10: 5-10. They were to be among the people, proclaiming the Gospel, serving the people, and conducting holistic ministries.

4. make a greater commitment to doing "good works" as noted in Matthew 5:13-16, and praying (1 Timothy 2: 1, 8).

5. re-appraise the immoral condition of the world and times in which we live as noted in 2 Timothy 3:1-5; and

make a recommitment to preaching and teaching the whole counsel of the Word.

6. Become more aware of, and engaged in spiritual warfare, in order to accomplish the work of God, and complete the kingdom mission (Ephesians 6:10-18). Just as the unjust laws of segregation and discrimination practices that held blacks down in Selma were not broken down without a fight, and death for some. Satan and the kingdom of darkness will not release people from the grips of sin, immorality, worldliness, greed and oppression and allow us to build Bible-centered, movement focused, holistic serving churches without a fight.

7. Take the dangerous step to re-examine the entire operation and organization, and be willing to change anything that needs to be changed in order to be more effective in completing the work of Christ before He returns. Continue preaching the Word of God because it is the only antidote to the continuing moral decaying of society (2 Timothy 4:1-5).

8. The most difficult aspect of the American church to deal with is the "money issue." Too many pastors, good men of God are too vested financially in the way our churches have operated for decades to get out or make drastic changes. Money is necessary to do ministry, and hardworking pastors and church staff people deserve to be paid, and have the means to support their families. Unfortunately money has become the driving force of too many churches. For this reason, I believe that one of the keys to spiritual revival in America is that new pastors and new churches must be trained to view and

use money differently. I am convinced that the current "made in America" brand of "capitalistic Christianity," that we have been practicing for decades will not be effective in reaching substantial numbers of unchurched people for Christ (Matthew 6:24, 1 Timothy 6: 6-10).

9. Established churches and their leadership will probably find it difficult, if not impossible to make the kind of changes suggested here. Therefore, I believe a better solution is for established churches to launch and support new churches, and new outreach ministries without upsetting or unnecessarily disrupting their current church operations. Many older leaders and church members probably cannot handle these kinds of drastic changes.

Lessons Learned

The primary issue I had to settle before I left my career in 1978 for full-time ministry was "the money issue." I had to decide how much I was going to allow money to control me and what I did or did not do for Christ. I have had to repeatedly revisit this issue over the years, and re-settle it in my life. Christians and ministers who are too attached or too dependent on money will automatically limit who they serve, and what types of ministries they will do for Christ.

My Hope and Prayer is that the people of God, and the local churches across America will wake-up, stand-up, and step-up to help stop the moral and spiritual decline that is currently happening in America.

References

I want to give credit to the following authors whose books were used as references, though no actual quotes were taken from the books.

Taylor Branch, *Parting the Waters –America in the King Years, 1954-63, Simon* and Schuster, 1988

J.L. Chestnut, Jr & Julia Cass, *Black in Selma – The Uncommon Life of J.L. Chestnut, Jr*, Farrar, Straus & Giroux, 1990

John Lewis with Michael D'orso, *Walking with the Wind – A Memoir of the Movement*, a Harvest Book, Harcourt Brace & Company, 1998

Andrew Young, *An Easy Burden – The Civil Rights Movement and the Transformation of America*, Harper Collins Publishers, 1996

From Selma to Salvation

From Selma to Salvation

www.ingramcontent.com/pod-product-compliance
Lightning Source LLC
Chambersburg PA
CBHW071004040426

42443CB00007B/653